25 years ago . . .

I reflected back on my remarkable dad.
The impact he had on my life.

The example he set.
His best advice.

I started sharing this with my sons.
I took them back in time.

My adventures with Dad.
What I learned.

They couldn't get enough.
And it taught them so much.

So I asked others about their dads.
Most were eager to share.

That's what this is—

How Fathers Change Lives
memories from daughters & sons
Stories of Remarkable Dads

Praise for
How Fathers Change Lives

"Greg Hague has captured remarkable lessons that will benefit every child and inspire every father to be the best he can be. These real-life reminiscences hit close to home for me. I still rely on advice my father gave me many years ago! Every dad, young and old, will learn from this book."

— HARVEY MACKAY
Author of the *New York Times* #1 bestseller,
Swim With The Sharks Without Being Eaten Alive

"Everyone wants to love their dad and see him in the best possible light. Reading this book will cause you to think about and appreciate your dad in ways you never considered. You are going to love this book!"

— MARK VICTOR HANSEN
Co-author of *Chicken Soup for the Soul*, motivational speaker, and owner of Hansen House Publishing

"I am so excited about this book. It was so needed. America's best dads. What they do. What they say. The lessons we learn. The difference they make. These stories remind us of the importance of our heritage and the impact fathers have on our lives. At no time in history have we needed strong, impactful fathers more than now. This book is a must-read. For all dads. For kids of all ages. *How Fathers Change Lives*—how true!"

— TOM HOPKINS
Bestselling author and speaker,
and America's foremost sales trainer

"*How Fathers Change Lives* touches on the profound effect our fathers have on us all and how they shape who we are today. The collection of anecdotes Greg Hague has put together are heartwarming and unforgettable. If you are a huge fan of the *Chicken Soup for The Soul* series, put it down immediately, and start reading *How Fathers Change Lives*. You will be moved, touched, and inspired after reading this incredible book."

—BRANDON STEINER
Founder and CEO of Steiner Sports

"This is so good I get emotional reading it. This will be as big as the *Chicken Soup* series. You also honor our Heavenly Father with your efforts. Remember, He is watching and you are making Him proud!"

—RITA DAVENPORT
Seminar leader, award-winning keynote speaker,
humorist, and author

"Fathers are the bedrock to children as families are to our country. Your vision is spectacular and your gift exceptional in capturing the richness of these unique men. Your writings will impact lives for generations to come."

—DAVE McLURG
CEO, Ignite International Corporation

"Our society needs to hear more stories like these of great dads being a positive influence and role model for their kids. Read this book and be inspired to be a better father!"

—LARRY WINGET
Television personality and author of five bestselling books, including
Your Kids Are Your Own Fault

How
FATHERS
CHANGE
LIVES

52 Stories from Kids of All Ages

GREG HAGUE

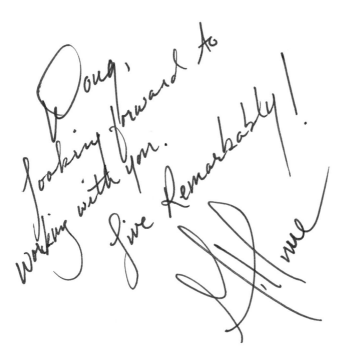

Doug,
Looking forward to
working with you.
Live Remarkably!

Contents

Harold "Chubby" Hague

Introduction

It's really dumb to think you're smart.

It was the afternoon of November 1st, 1980. I had just sold my son's winter jacket at a yard sale for $6.00. I needed the money.

My business had flopped. My home had been sold. I lost everything. Ego shattered. Life as I knew it had ended.

It was horribly embarrassing, but 100% my fault. I had been living an illusion.

With an elite law school education, I thought I was incredibly smart. My ego agreed. Then, I got toasted by a competitor who made a wicked-smart move. Remember the movie *Top Gun*? My ego wrote checks my smarts couldn't cash.

I was a beat-up example of the difference between being educated and being smart.

My dad, "Chubby," came to the rescue—not with money, but with savvy. He told me what happened and explained why. I came back big.

Chubby taught me what to do when, when to say what, and when to shut up. He taught me things that others seemed not to know. It made me millions, set me free, and made my life.

After my sons were born, I so wanted to be a great dad. It was my #1 priority in life. So I looked back on how my dad had helped me. Our adventures together, our father-son talks, his savvy advice, and the example he set.

I began sharing Chubby stories with my sons—our most memorable times, what I learned, how it helped me in life.

My boys were intrigued. They begged for more. Chubby's lessons on life became the hot topic at dinner and during long car trips.

What happened next? My sons started telling Chubby stories to their friends. Those friends began sharing stories about their dads. It didn't take long before their dads were telling stories about their dads.

Soon I was flooded with story after story of remarkable fathering. It became a way to honor the men who shaped our lives, and a bible on how to be a great dad.

That's why I created this book—to share stories about remarkable dads. Best times. Best adventures. Best advice. It's a place to pay tribute. A place to see how others parent their kids.

Each story is told from the look-back perspective of a daughter or son. "What my dad did. What my dad said. How he impacted my life."

It's the best of great dads through the lens of their kids.

—Greg Hague

> *"Don't feel entitled to anything you
> didn't sweat and struggle for."*
>
> Marian Wright Edelman

– 1 –

Two-Hatted Dad

contributed by Tom Leonard

My dad wears two hats. It started like this.

"Tom, join me in the hot tub. Let's talk," said Dad. Pretty cool, I thought. Hot tubbin' with dad. A father-son chat. Why not?

And, I was due for a raise. I'd worked at Dad's store for months. He took me on when I quit college. Dad wasn't pleased when I bailed out of school, but he swallowed hard and gave me a job. That worked for me. I needed the bucks.

My name is Tom Leonard. My dad is Stewart Leonard. He's quite a guy.

My father started his business in 1969. Back then it was a small dairy store with seven employees. It's now the "World's Largest Dairy Store" with 2,000 members of our multi-store team.

College was boring. That's why I quit. Because of my father's success, I figured I pretty much had it made.

I'd been working for months in the store. "Start at the bottom," Dad said. So I did. Stocking the shelves. Sweeping up. That was my gig.

One day the phone rang. Great news. All my buddies were headed to Ft. Lauderdale for Easter Break. Heck, I thought, I'd been working hard. I needed a break.

I asked Mr. Barry, our store manager, if I could take a few days off.

I could hardly believe what he said!

Mr. Barry was nice, but firm. The answer was no. Something about the busy Easter weekend. He needed my help.

"No?" I thought. "I'm the boss's son. My dad owns the place. I don't have to listen to that." So I took off.

Tom Leonard and his father, Stewart

Man, what a blast. My friends and I showed that Florida town what fun's all about.

So now back to that hot tub with Dad. I arrived with a smile (and a tan from my trip). I shucked off my jeans and pulled on my shorts.

My father was waiting, submerged to his shoulders. I plopped into the tub. Pretty cool! Just me and dad. This was good, I thought. "So what's up, Dad?" I asked.

Here's what he said, "You know, Tom, being a father and a boss in a family business is a tough job. I have to wear two hats."

Dad turned and reached behind him. He picked up a red baseball cap and placed it on his head. He said, "Tom, on the one hand, I'm your dad."

Tom never forgot the advice he received from his father the businessman, or the support from his father the dad. His two-hatted dad helped him achieve great success.

Dad then turned, removed the red hat, grabbed a white one from the ledge, and put it squarely on his head. He said, "On the other hand, I'm also the boss. As the boss, I have to treat all of my employees fairly.

"Your manager told me you asked for vacation. He said no. You didn't listen. You went anyway.

"I hope you understand that I have to treat you just the same as our other employees. So Tom, you're fired."

My mind went instantly blank. Fired by Dad? How would I live? Where would I work? I had quit school and had no real skills.

But Dad wasn't through. What did he do?

My father proceeded to take off that white "boss hat" and put the red "dad hat" back on.

He said, "Son, I hear you just lost your job. What can I do to help?"

Tom Leonard at his Farmer's Market

With Dad's help and encouragement, I went back to college. I earned my degree and now operate my very own place. Come by and say hi. It's Tom Leonard's Farmer's Market in Richmond, Virginia. It's thanks to my dad.

ABOUT THE CONTRIBUTOR

Tom Leonard is the founder of Tom Leonard's Farmer's Market. His store has been recognized by *Richmond Guide* as #1 in the "Top 15 Things to Do with Kids" in Richmond. *Richmond Magazine* named it #1 in the "50 Best Food Finds" in Richmond and the #1 place to purchase produce.

> *"If you live to be a hundred, I want to live
> to be a hundred minus one day so I never have to
> live without you."*
>
> From *Winnie-The-Pooh*, by A.A. Milne

– 2 –

Finding a Ralph

contributed by Lise Johnson

They were married 48 years.

Mom became terminally ill. The road to the end was brutal and long. Dad stopped work and stayed home. Caring for Mom was a full-time job. His business folded. We lived off savings.

Mom loved it at home. She wanted to spend her last days surrounded by family, memories, and the things she knew. Dad would have it no other way.

Friends pitched in to help, but Dad was "on duty" 'round the clock. In the final two weeks, we moved her to hospice. She needed professional care.

Joyce and Ralph's marriage was filled with laughter and love

Dad slept there. Ate there. Ensured Mom was warm. He held her hand while she slept.

I'd urge Dad, "Go home. Take a break." I had to kick him out just to go home and clean up. Dad did not want Mom to spend one single minute alone.

When the final moment arrived, Dad knelt next to Mom's bed. He knew. She knew. Her hand was cupped gently in his.

It hurt badly to see Mom go. But it helped to see the devotion, the love, and the remarkable care she received from my dad. Others throughout the hospice saw it, as well.

"Your dad's devotion," said one nurse wistfully.

"Never in all my years," a doctor shared.

And then something happened that changed my perspective on love, on life. A nurse who had spent considerable time with Mom approached me. I can still see her face clearly.

"Lise," she said, "I have something to share. I was engaged when I started your mom's care. "No longer," she continued. When I expressed sympathy, she interrupted.

"Lise, don't be sorry. I'm not. This was my choice. My man was no match for your dad, Ralph.

"I didn't know devotion like that existed in this world. I decided I would wait until I could find a man like your dad.

"I want a Ralph."

Lise Johnson is an Executive Editor at John Wiley & Sons Publishing (Hoboken, New Jersey). Lise's mother, Joyce, passed away in 2007. Dad Ralph goes to their church each day to "visit" her.

He carries her photo wherever he goes.

Lise in 2013 with her new husband, Robert Webb. Lise found her "Ralph."

> *"Losers make promises they often break.*
> *Winners make commitments they always keep."*
>
> Denis Waitley

– 3 –

Best Prom Never

contributed by Randy Garn

Young Randy Garn with Mom and Dad, years before the night that changed his life

I had just turned 16. I had a date, and asked Dad if I could borrow the car.

He said, "Okay, but I want you home by 11:00," handing over the keys. "We have fences to mend, cows to milk, and crops to tend. We start sharply at 5:00. I need you bright and on beam."

I promised I'd be home right on the dot. Dad said my upcoming prom was at stake should I be late.

That night was so fun. I lost track of the time! Well, actually, no. I knew I was staying out too late. All right, I thought. I'll sneak quietly in; I just won't get caught.

So I snuck through the door at 1:16 a.m. (I remember the time to this day). I knew I'd be in trouble if Dad found out. I gently laid the keys on the table, nary a sound.

Without squeaking a board, so light on my feet, I tiptoed upstairs and slid quickly into my room.

With a sigh of relief, I told myself it was okay, all was just right. I shed my clothes in a pile, pulled back the covers and slid under the sheets.

My heart leapt into my throat. I sprang up with a start. A nightmare for sure! Under the covers. Waiting for me. Coach Garn. My dad.

"What time did I say to be home?" he asked, firm but quite calm. I admitted it was 1:17. I had broken my word.

His next words, spoken without anger, would prove that my coach and my dad was a man of his word. He expected no less of his son.

"I'm not mad," said Dad, "but the prom is now gone. Randy, I love you so much, but unlike what you did tonight, I do what I say. You must learn to live your life that way."

Coach Nyle Garn's words shaped his son's life, and today the two men love spending time together

I don't know why, but I felt this was a night that would shape the rest of my days. I made up my mind that no matter how much effort, how great the sacrifice, I would be like my father, I would keep my word and do what I say.

Dad and I knelt down to pray.

That night set the path of my life. Responsibility. Accountability. Honor promises. Do what I say.

It sounds easy. We all know it's not. When my way is unclear, I reflect back to that memorable night. I learned from a man who says what is right and does what he says. Coach Garn. Because of Dad, I do what I say.

ABOUT THE CONTRIBUTOR

Randy Garn is a Harvard alum, bestselling author, and Entrepreneur of the Year. Randy's global coaching firm, Prosper, Inc., is tops in the world.

Randy Garn and his dad, Nyle, with bestselling author, Harvey Mackay

It was Randy's father, Coach Nyle Garn, who taught Randy how to coach others in life. For over 26 years, he coached his high school football teams to #1 in Northern Idaho. His players still adore this big-hearted, very tough guy.

From football to fishing to fathering, Coach Nyle Garn does what he says

"I speak to everyone in the same way,
whether he is the garbage man
or the president of the university."

Albert Einstein

– 4 –

Mahogany Desk

contributed by Calvin LeHew

I was born above a small country store July 15, 1939, in Hillsboro, Tennessee. My parents worked into the night. Money was tight. The elementary school was without plumbing.

My dad, Alton "Red" LeHew, only finished third grade. My mom, Leola, made it through sixth. They both died of cancer when I was a kid.

Dad was without money. He was without education. The result? People often looked down on my father.

But Dad was determined to succeed. What he lacked in learning, he made up for with ambition and hard work. When Dad couldn't get a job at the local lumber mill, he showed up each day anyway. He worked without a paycheck so he could learn the lumber trade. He studied everything about that business.

After a couple years, Dad was ready to start his own small lumber yard. He went to the Williamson County

Bank for a $100 loan. He needed to finance a small tractor to move the logs.

The loan was perfectly safe. It was only $100. The tractor would secure the loan. Dad had lived in the community most of his life.

But there was a problem. My father was on the weak side of the mahogany desk. He really needed that loan.

The bank officer stared coldly at Dad from the strong side of the mahogany. He cavalierly replied, "No."

But Dad didn't give up. Eventually, he opened his own lumber yard, and then a gas station, too.

Because Dad, many times, had been on the weak side of a mahogany desk, he constantly warned me, "Don't look down on anybody—ever." (He knew firsthand how that felt.)

Alton "Red" LeHew with his son, Calvin. The year? Long ago.

"Treat everyone like the most important person in the world, because someday you may have to walk up to that person's mahogany desk and ask for a job."

Dad hit the nail on the head. His advice influences how I treat each person, each day. To me, this is success principle #1.

Respect. Courtesy. They matter to me. I focus on those two words with everyone I meet. Mahogany desk? The person on the weak side today may own it tomorrow. (He was right.)

Remember the bank in Williamson that turned Dad down? I became a director.

The mahogany was mine. I did it for Dad.

ABOUT THE CONTRIBUTOR

From humble beginnings, Calvin LeHew rose to the top. He worked for Presidents Nixon, Kennedy, and Johnson. One of his youthful goals was to make his first million by age 35. He did it at 33.

What advice meant the most?

Words from his dad ... mahogany desk.

> *"Courage is not the absence of fear, but rather the judgment that something is more important than fear."*
>
> James Neil Hollingsworth

– 5 –

Special Skin

contributed by Jason Fields

I didn't have a dad growing up. Mom raised me, for the most part.

I did have an uncle. His name was Greg. Uncle Greg taught me something special about me.

It was 1981, another bleak, freezing Cincinnati winter.

My name is Jason. I was five at the time. The memory is vivid, even today. Standing in the Cincinnati Kmart. Longingly gazing at the most beautiful thing I had ever seen, a jet black Huffy Panther BMX bicycle.

Chrome spokes, riding pegs, trick handlebars, and "panther claw" grips! My heart pounded at the thought of riding this powerful steed.

But then came the fear—no training wheels.

My friend, Gatsby, was already riding without 'em. He'd taken a nasty spill the week before. Scraped knee. Bloody shin. Tears.

Cousins Brian and Jason, not quite ready for two wheels

Not for me! But the thought of furiously screaming around corners consumed me. A Panther for Christmas! It would be mine.

As the big day approached, fear overwhelmed. I regretted my passionate plea to Santa just a month before. I needed an escape! Quick, write Santa. Change my order to Legos this year. Yep, Legos. Safe play.

Uncle Greg had just flown back from Phoenix for Christmas that year. I think Mom ratted me out.

"So, Jason, I hear you want Legos instead of the Panther?"

I couldn't show fear, not with Uncle Greg. "Oh, I already have a bike, Uncle Greg. But I really need more Legos." Quick thinking, I thought.

The Huffy Panther BMX bicycle—a young boy's dream

Uncle Greg raised an eyebrow, smiled, and said, "Well, I hope Santa comes through." Threw him off. Good job, I told myself.

Christmas morning. The truth? I hated myself. Coward was me. Gatsby would be zipping around. I'd still be "in training," creeping along.

Breakfast casserole. Baileys and coffee this one day of the year. Time for presents. Yep, there they were. Legos, wrapped in a box. Disappointed with myself, I trudged up the stairs. Soon, Gatsby would call, wanting to ride. My head in my pillow, I started to cry.

"Jason, come down here," Uncle Greg yelled from below. "I need help in the barn."

I slowly walked down the stairs, and there, in front of the fire, angled just so, leaning on its stand, black paint glistening—The Panther.

Dumbfounded, I looked around. Big, beaming smiles everywhere, and then I broke down.

"No!" I said, "I'll crash. I'll rip off my skin. I'll be covered with blood."

All faces went straight. I raced up the stairs. My pillow was warm and wet from before. I sobbed so hard my ribs ached.

Then, a knock at the door. "Can I come in?" Uncle Greg asked.

"I don't care," I sniffed.

"Jason, it's time to tell you a family secret."

I was intrigued. I turned and peeked up at Greg.

"We have something called special skin. Did you know?" I shook my head, "No."

"Our family has a special type of skin. When we're injured, it only hurts half as bad. And, it heals twice as fast."

Could this be? A family secret? Why hadn't someone told me?

"Jason, you will probably fall. When you do, remember, you have special skin. It won't hurt that bad."

Soon, Uncle Greg was watching me do figure eights on that Panther. Did I fall? Yes. But it only hurt half as bad.

We aren't born brave. Courage is learned. Fear is a liar. Worry is waste.

All kids have special skin. Let them know.

About the Contributor

Jason Fields is a manager for Apollo Education Services. He lives in Scottsdale, Arizona, and has proudly graduated from that Huffy Panther to a Subaru STI. The author's nephew, Jason is considered a fourth son.

"People focus on role models; it is more effective to find anti-models—people you don't want to resemble when you grow up."

From Nassim Nicholas Taleb's *The Black Swan*

– 6 –

The Me I Did Not Want to Be

by Greg Hague

Are you happy with who you are?

It was a Saturday breakfast with Dad at Perkins Pancake House in Montgomery, Ohio. I was 12, maybe 13. It was our father-son tradition—the highlight of my week for years. We sat across from each other in a dark red, shiny booth next to the window, looking out at the road. It was a cold, icy morning. I had just ordered my usual ... pancakes, hash browns, and a double order of crispy bacon.

As we casually chatted about my week at school, my grades, cute girls, and such, Dad discreetly nodded and asked me to look around the restaurant at the diverse groups of people at each table.

He then asked, "Greg, do you ever think about who you don't want to be?"

"What do you mean?" I asked.

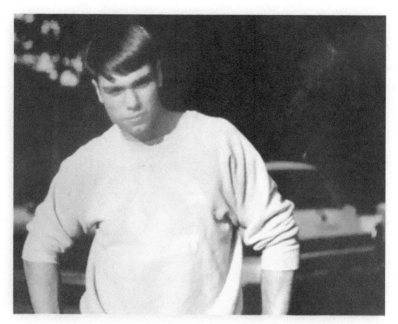

Greg Hague, just a few years ago

"I mean," he continued, "do you ever think about who you would most *not* like to be like when you grow up?"

It didn't take long. I named names. With each person, Dad would ask why. After I explained, he would say something like, "How exactly do you think they ended up that way?" We each gave our opinion. It became a game of how *not* to make it in life.

Lack of effort? No self-discipline? C's in school? Eating too much? Afraid to go for it? Worried about looking bad?

Dad even asked if perhaps these people had just meandered through life with no clear vision of what they wanted to be. He suggested that maybe they hadn't done anything wrong.

Chubby Hague, Greg's dad, spoke words that would help set the course of his son's life

He said, "*Wrong* presumes they tried to be something more. Many don't."

We had previously talked a lot about how to make it in life. We had never discussed how I might look back, disappointed with mine. It was scary. Toward the end of our discussion, Chubby asked me a piercing question.

"Greg," he said, "right now, are you happy with what you've so far accomplished in your life?"

I knew the answer was no. I envied my friends who had better grades, played better ball, or headed a club. It wasn't that I couldn't do what they'd done. I just hadn't. I didn't have the courage to tell my father.

Dad taught me a lot. Often, at the time, I didn't realize the importance of his lessons. This time, I did. When my father asked me if I was satisfied with "me," it really drove the point home.

I had never considered how easy it would be to mess up my life. In the car on the way home, I remember thinking, "I am not going to become a me I do not want to be!"

Right: Greg
and date at
a costume
Deb Dance,
16 years old
(DEFINITELY
NOT the ME
I wanted to be)

Below:
Cousin Jeff
with Greg
at 11 on
Walloon
Lake,
Michigan

Deb Dance

AT "THE LAST HURRAH," Mr. and Mrs. John
Wood II's debut costume dance, Friday, their
daughter, Crystie, symbolizes movie "Screen
Gems" and Gregory Hague is "The Carpet
Bagger."

Photos by Julianne Warren

> *"My education was interrupted only by my schooling."*
>
> Winston Churchill

– 7 –

Later is Now

contributed by Katie McDevitt

School was out! I hopped on the bus headed for home.

A young lady of 10, I was anxious to play outside with my friends.

As we rounded the corner, my house appeared. Something was wrong. I squished my face tight to the glass. In the front lawn, my little red bike.

I could hardly believe what I saw. Standing up in the yard, a "For Sale" sign tied to the bars.

For sale? I thought. My red bike was my life, my escape after school.

What had I done? Remember, I was just 10. Imagine if someone had taken and sold off your car.

I jumped off the bus. Ran 'cross the yard. Flew into the house.

I zipped past my dad (with him I was mad). I flew into the kitchen, straight to my mom. "He's selling my bike!" I fitfully sobbed.

"Well, why would he do that?" Mom sympathetically asked. I shrugged (with my best 10-year-old innocent look).

Uh oh, I suddenly thought. Behind me, a squeak on the floor. I knew who it was. Dad had walked into the room.

"Katie, four weeks ago you borrowed $20. You wanted to buy extra snacks. I told you lenders expect interest and payback. We agreed to 16%. You understood, right?"

Yes, I nodded. This was not good.

"And, I explained about liens. Your bike would be used to pay off the loan if you did not. Did you understand?" I nodded my head.

"It's been four weeks. I'm here to collect."

I remembered the day I asked for that loan. I wanted the $20 "now." Four weeks seemed far down the road.

Crazy, I thought, it's amazing how fast later is now.

Katie, her mom, Ellen, and their dog, Keeley

I needed a plan. My bike was at stake. Odd jobs? A loan from my mom? I was thinking hard and fast.

Then I briefly looked up. What was this? An ear-to-ear grin on Dad's face? With a twinkle in his eye, he gave me a playful nudge, a kiss on the head, and a father's advice,

"Katie, here are four lessons schools don't teach:

- Don't make deals you can't keep.
- Don't take out loans for frivolous things.
- Interest is your enemy.
- And, it's amazing how fast later is now.

Now go out and have fun on your bike."

ABOUT THE CONTRIBUTOR

Katie McDevitt is Jim Reid's loving daughter. To this day she strives to follow her father's advice.

Katie grew up in Phoenix, Arizona, and now resides in San Francisco, California. She is a Santa Clara grad, and is

Katie and her dad, Jim Reid. Jim Reid passed away in March 2006 from kidney failure at age 45. Even though Katie wasn't ready to live life without her dad, he had done an incredible job preparing her and her brother, Ryan, for lifelong success.

Vice President at Guy Carpenter & Company. In 2012 she married the love of her life and future savvy dad, Mookie McDevitt.

"Miracles come in moments.
Be ready and willing."

Wayne Dyer

– 8 –

A Special Appreciation for Living

contributed by Janie Hite

My name is Janie Hite. I am four, a big girl now. Thanks to my dad and another kind man, I'm alive today.

I was born with serious problems most babies don't have. The medical terms don't matter—they're just big words. With some luck and good care, I'll be fine.

I won't grow up to typical height. I'll look a bit different. But I can live a long, happy life.

When I was two, I almost died. Two men saved my life—Dr. Ben Carson and my dad.

"Emergency surgery," the doctors exclaimed. The problem? Something scary called "water on the brain." I needed a difficult operation few knew how to do. I needed it right then to keep me alive.

My dad flew into action. He learned that one man in the country was my best hope. His name? Dr. Ben Carson. The problem? He is a busy, important man. Few can even reach him.

Dr. Ben Carson is Director of Pediatric Neurosurgery at Johns Hopkins Hospital. President Bush gave him the Presidential Medal of Freedom in 2008. That is the highest civilian award in the U.S. Some even tell Dr. Carson he should run for President. He'd sure have my vote!

John, Kristen, and Janie Hite with Dr. Ben Carson

It was a long shot, but my father was determined to reach Dr. Carson—even in the middle of the night. So at 2:00 in the morning, a few hours before my surgery, Dad sent him an urgent email.

Dr. Carson later told us "something" caused him to awake at that early hour. He checked the email on his phone and saw the note from my dad.

Even though he had two other surgeries that morning, he reviewed my records, spoke with my dad, advised the doctors on my surgery, took me as a patient and personally performed another serious surgery I needed a few months later.

After I was feeling better, we asked Dr. Carson, "What do you think woke you so early, made you check your email, and decide to help?" He pointed his finger up to the sky. All I know is that without that nice Dr. Ben Carson and my amazing dad, I wouldn't be here today.

Just watch me. I'm going to grow up to do special things. My path may be a bit tougher than most, but that's okay. It will make me strong. For my age, I think it already has.

My dad says difficult hurdles give us an appreciation for living others don't have. I'm learning he's right.

ABOUT THE CONTRIBUTOR

Janie Hite lives in Virginia with her parents, John and Kristin, her brother, Benjamin, and her sisters, Mary Katelyn and

Lauren. She loves coloring, drawing, going to the beach, and riding ponies with her instructor. A busy girl, Janie especially enjoys her many friends in her pre-kindergarten and gymnastics/dance classes.

Janie with Dad, John

> *"The way to gain a good reputation is to endeavor to be what you desire to appear."*
>
> Socrates

– 9 –

Apology Letters

contributed by Casey Hague

Casey Hague, 1989

As a child, I was "independent." Trouble, some said.

Kindergarten, first grade, second grade, my tidbits of terror were becoming well known—until the apology letter.

Second grade. Mrs. Robinson's class. Report card day. I was eight.

Report cards at this level were not letter grades, but O (outstanding), S (satisfactory), or N (not good)—indicators to parents of what was to come.

I thought nothing of it. Didn't even look.

I walked into the house and tossed the report card on the table. Time for some skateboard action outside.

"Casey, come in here," I heard Dad yell.

I sauntered back into the house. Dad looked upset.

"Sit down," he said, pointing to a kitchen chair. "Did you see this report card?"

The tone. The look. I'd seen it before. Dad was mad.

"Uh, no Dad, I thought it was for parents," I said with a look of feigned innocence.

Dad sternly said, "Casey, you need to understand about grades in this family."

"Okay," I said.

"O's are expected, S's unacceptable, and N's are punishable. Your grades are all S's and N's. This will never happen again.

"You are grounded for two weeks. Now go upstairs and write an apology letter to Mrs. Robinson for not trying your best."

Casey and his dad, Greg, at Disney's Haunted Mansion

"But Dad ... "

He cut me off, "And Casey, if you ever get an S or an N again, you will be grounded until the next report card. You won't leave this house. You are more than capable. I expect all O's from now on."

I burst into tears, ran upstairs, and slammed my door.

Later that night, Dad asked me to stay at the dinner table.

"Casey, you are the smartest kid in your class; you know it and so do I. Right?"

I nodded. I didn't "know" this, but it sounded great!

"I love that you want to stand out," Dad said. "But there's doing it wrong and doing it right. Starting tonight, you're going to understand right."

Dad continued, "From now on, when you're bad, I'm not going to yell, I won't even be mad. You will simply write an apology letter to any adult who sees what you did. And

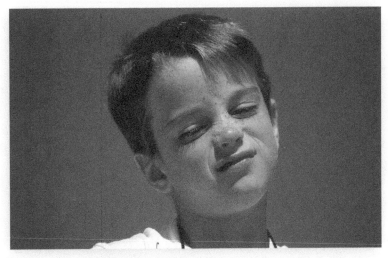

Casey with a little "attitude"

I'm going to ask them all—your mom, your teacher, my friends—to watch you extra close and to let me know."

I complained. I said no. But I knew Dad. He made things like this a big deal. He'd be watching me, looking for chances to make me write those letters.

That night Dad helped me write the apology to my teacher. There were many more to come in the weeks and months ahead.

What happened?

People started to write back. They said really nice things. My reputation started to change. So did I.

I started to believe Dad may have been right—perhaps I *was* a smart kid.

It was a bumpy road, but when I finally took hold, Dad said, "Casey, I always knew you would turn out to be great—one of the world's greatest criminals, or one of its greatest successes. I was right!"

Greg and Casey, the next morning in LaJolla, after Casey passed the difficult California bar exam

Where am I now? This weekend, Dad flew to California to be at my side. It was a huge moment in my life.

Last night, the results were posted. Together we logged into the California Bar Exam website.

Tears flooded my eyes, and Dad's too. We hugged. Great night.

Now I'll be putting those letter-writing skills to good use—for clients in my legal practice.

ABOUT THE CONTRIBUTOR

Casey Hague is now 30, and just passed the California Bar Exam. He lives in San Diego, and works for a firm that negotiates complex easements and leases for cell phone towers.

*"Just do what must be done. This may not be
happiness, but it is greatness."*
George Bernard Shaw

– 10 –

Just Do What Has to Be Done

contributed by Darren Hardy

My dad would have been 66 years old yesterday. I lost him to bone cancer seven months ago.

In his eulogy I passed forward the half-dozen philosophies he taught me that shaped me into the man I am today, in the hope they might benefit those in attendance. In honor and celebration of his birthday, I'd like to pass one of those philosophies forward to you.

This one saved my life ... and defined my life.

You might know that my parents divorced when I was only 18 months old. My mother never really wanted to be a mother (she got angry when she found out she was pregnant with me), so when they split up, she cheerfully handed me over to my dad.

My dad didn't know what to do with me either. He was only 23 years old when I was born. He had just moved from his hometown, in the San Francisco Bay Area, to what seemed like the middle of nowhere in Albuquerque, New Mexico. There we were, out there all alone.

The Hardy boys

When this all came down, my dad's mother (my grandmother) insisted that he ship me home to her. He said no. So she got on a plane and showed up on his front doorstep, further insisting. This was a dramatic act, because she was scared to death to fly, had never been on a plane before and probably never flew again thereafter.

He once again said no, which was hard for him because his mother ruled his world. He always did what she insisted. Not this time. He told her he was committed to do what he had to do.

We then moved to Hawaii, where my dad was the football coach for the University of Hawaii. A year later his mother died suddenly of a heart attack. His father was not dealing with it well, and he feared for his life. My dad left his coaching position and moved us back to the Bay Area and in with my grandfather.

My dad now had to look for another job. There were not many coaching jobs to be had. Many months went by and the situation was getting dire. Finally, a head coaching job (a dream job for my dad) opened up at Olympic College in Washington. There were three guys in the running. The other two were more qualified than my dad, but he out-hustled and out-charmed them.

The day finally came for a decision, and the phone rang. It was the chancellor of the college, and he had the entire board of 40 people in the room with him. With lots of hoopla, they announced that my dad was being awarded the position as the new head football coach of Olympic College. My dad replied that he would need to call them back; he needed to talk with his father first. The chancellor said they would all stay in the room and wait while he did so.

By that time, my grandfather was not doing well over the loss of my grandmother. He was drinking during the day, which he never did, and was going to bed with his clothes still on and showing up to work in them the next day.

When my dad told his father about the job offer in Washington, my grandfather's eyes welled up with tears and he said, "Just do what you have to do, son."

My dad picked up the phone and called back the chancellor. He said, "I have to decline your offer. I have to take care of my dad." There was dead silence for five seconds or more. Then one person in a distant part of the room clapped. Then the room erupted in applause. He hung the phone up and never looked back.

Today I applaud my dad one more time. Because when it came down to it, he just did what had to be done. And because he did, I have the life I have today. And because he did, I hope that maybe today, yesterday or tomorrow I can have an impact on your life in some way. If that happens, then my dad lives on.

About the Contributor

Darren Hardy is publisher and editorial director of *SUCCESS* magazine. He has been a leader in the per-sonal development industry for 17 years, having led two personal development-based television networks and published two bestselling books, *The Compound Effect* and *Living Your Best Year Ever*. He has mentored thousands of entrepreneurs and advised many large corporations. He sits on the board of several companies and nonprofit organizations.

Darren regularly appears on national radio and TV shows for CNBC, MSNBC, CBS, ABC, and FOX.

Darren currently resides in Cardiff-by-the-Sea (San Diego), California, with his wife, Georgia, and his canine children, Lucy and Tex.

"The best thing to spend on your children is time."
Arnold Glasow

– II –

Kidnapped by Dad
contributed by Mort Dukehart

"Pack your bags. We're taking a weekend trip."

Virtually every weekend, my brother and I took a trip with Dad. Sometimes near, often far. We piled in the car. Off we went.

We never knew where until we arrived. It might be just a few hours. It could be days. It was always a surprise.

Even on a rare weekend at home, Dad took us on long walks to pick up driftwood from Long Island Sound or a short drive to check out new local sites.

The Dukehart boys were doers, not observers. Dad wanted us to learn the world by experiencing it. And he loved to spend time with his boys. We felt the same about him.

"Where are we going this weekend, Dad?" asked my brother and me. Dad's answer was always the same, "It's a surprise, boys, we'll just have to see."

We were lucky. We lived near New York City— endless opportunities, emblems of every part of the world close at hand.

Above: a weekend adventure with Dad

Left: the young Dukehart brothers

The Museum of Natural History. Chinatown. The Bronx Botanical Gardens. Little Italy. Coney Island and its Aquarium. The United Nations or Yankee Stadium to see the New York Giants play. We watched the West Point cadets walk in their parade and play lacrosse.

Best of all was when Dad would say, "Pack your bags. We're taking a weekend trip this time."

The anticipation was palpable. We drove, often for hours, toward our next surprise. Dad usually kept it a secret until we arrived.

Roadside diners. Motels with their humming neon signs. Their floors creaking with mystery.

What my brother and I learned on those trips went beyond what we experienced and saw. The conversations were like a "University of Dad."

Our father shared tales of triumph, stories of loss, practical tips, savvy and smarts. Each trip was a primer on life.

These days, kids get around easily, often with friends— but in the 1950s, travel was harder. You needed a dad. Today, time with our fathers, adventures alone with our dads, seem to have faded away.

Mort's travels with his father—to places like Gettysburg and Monticello—inspired a love of history

Baseball Hall of Fame. The Gettysburg Battlefield. Thomas Jefferson's house at Monticello ... magic to me. And they planted the seed for my passion for history. It's how I make my living today—a teacher of history, now a principal of schools. Like Dad, I spend my time igniting passions in young minds.

I reflect back on those trips, the talks, those special experiences with Dad. What did I learn? What is my advice for the fathers out there?

Quality time with Dad breeds curious boys into quality men.

ABOUT THE CONTRIBUTOR

Mort Dukehart is the Head of the Middle School at Phoenix Country Day School in Paradise Valley, Arizona.

He is probably the biggest Baltimore Colts fan in the world.

Mort with daughter, Jacquie, and grandson, Graham

*"Don't wanna cry anymore,
so may I stay with you?
And he said, 'That's my job ...
to keep you safe with me.'"*

"That's My Job," written by Hap Hall,
performed by Conway Twitty

– 12 –

Daddies Never Go Away

contributed by Michael Twitty

His life was cut short in 1993 at just 59.

Harold Lloyd Jenkins shaped music history.

Never heard of him? Yes, you have. His stage name was Conway Twitty.

Conway reigned supreme in country music with 55 consecutive #1 records. He played with Elvis, Johnny Cash, and other legends at Sun Studios.

He reached into outer space when his famous hit "Hello Darlin'" was broadcast between American and Russian astronauts, a gesture of international goodwill.

But this is not about Conway, the star. It's about Conway, the dad.

Dad showed up at my door one night. He wore his favorite Mickey Mouse pj's. (If only his female fans could see him, I thought.)

In his hand he held a cassette. "'That's My Job' is the name of the song," Dad said. "I'm thinking of recording it. Won't you give it a listen, son?"

Dad popped it in my cassette player. We plopped down on the couch. We listened. It was to become a top hit. But here's the thing - I didn't like it. Not one bit.

"You don't like it?" he asked, looking perplexed. Dad was surprised. I'm also a musician. We had always shared the same tastes.

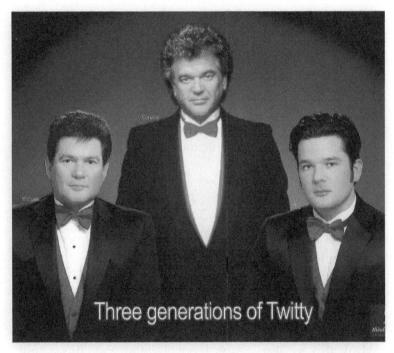

Conway Twitty (center), his son, Michael (left), and Michael's son, Tre

"Well Dad, to tell you the truth, it's the first time I've thought about life without you."

Dad fell quiet for a moment. He looked down at his slippers, "Boy, I'm about to let you in on one of life's great secrets:

"Daddies die. But they never go away.

"Wherever you are, whatever you do, whether I'm dead or alive, listen to this song and know I'm always with you."

The next six hours we spent on that couch. We talked until sunrise. Family. Love. Risk. Our dreams. We cried and we hugged. That song brought us closer than ever before.

Michael Twitty sharing a casual moment with his dad, Conway Twitty

Dad went on to record that song. It climbed the charts. It became an anthem for the bond between dads and their kids. It brought tears to millions of eyes, not just mine.

One last thing. What's it like to be Conway Twitty's son?

Proud. As proud as a boy can be.

But, as proud as I am to be the son of the music legend, Conway Twitty, I'm a thousand times more proud to be the son of the man, Harold Lloyd Jenkins. He was one of the finest human beings to walk the earth.

ABOUT THE CONTRIBUTOR

Michael Twitty is the oldest son of rock and country legend Conway Twitty. Like his dad, Michael is a talented, highly acclaimed entertainer. He has traveled the globe performing the dynamic "Michael Twitty Show," the "Memories of Conway Show," and the remarkable "Twitty Bird Show."

*"Fear makes strangers
of people who would be friends."*

Shirley MacLaine

– 13 –

Draw a Wider Circle

contributed by Lori Holden

My name is Lori. Today I'll share what may be the greatest life lesson in the history of humankind—spoken through the words of my Dad.

Want to have a richer life? Dad told us the secret early on,

"Draw a wider circle."

A bit anticlimactic, you say? Well, few words can speak great volumes. Let me explain.

I grew up with two sisters. Sometimes we came home whining, "The other kids won't play with me!" or "They're leaving me out!" or "Nobody likes me!"

Dad would always respond simply,

"Draw a wider circle."

He said it repeatedly, ad nauseum. Dad was big on aphorisms, but that's another story.

He suspected that, more often than not, we were actually excluding ourselves by making assumptions about others. He constantly reminded us that the other kids were scared of making new friends too, so we could choose to be the ones to approach them and join in on activities. Dad was determined to raise three confident and assertive young women.

As a kid, I couldn't comprehend the magnitude of impact this one phrase would have on the rest of my life. When I was the newbie at work gatherings, and surely everyone else already had friends, Dad's voice would whisper,

"Draw a wider circle."

And I would. Hand out, I'd introduce myself and smile. At cocktail parties, when I'd rather hug the wall than interrupt a formed group, Dad's voice echoed,

"Draw a wider circle"

And I did. I made friends. I was included.

Lori and her dad (both right), and the whole Holden family

Ever seen the movie *Field of Dreams* — the voice quietly urging Kevin Costner, "If you build it, they will come"? This was my dad's gift to us.

And true enough, my "field of dreams" was always within grasp, provided I listen to Dad's voice,

"Draw a wider circle."

I can't remember it *not* working. I do remember it being hard each and every time — but always worth it. It applies to a much greater concept though, circling back to the "greatest life lesson" reference.

When you force yourself to draw a wider circle, as uncomfortable as it may be, you automatically enrich your own life with the only thing in life that really matters — other people.

Drawing a wider circle means:

- Making an effort to reach out to those you may not get along with.

- Risking rejection to meet the one person who may sweep you off your feet.

- Overcoming the fear of joining new groups, trying things you never thought you would (or even could), and travelling to parts of the country and the world you never knew existed.

My dad grew up without a father. Maybe that forced him to "draw a wider circle" early on in life.

But for not having a dad growing up, he certainly didn't let that stop him from being the most incredible father any three little girls could ask for.

XOXO Dad. Thanks for loving us so well.

About the Contributor

Lori Holden writes regularly at *LavenderLuz.com* and is on Twitter as @LavLuz. Her book, *The Open-Hearted Way to Open Adoption: Helping Your Child Grow Up Whole,*  written with her daughter's birth mom, is available through your favorite online bookseller. She lives in Denver with her husband, Roger, and tweens, Tessa and Reed. These days she draws wider circles through her yoga practice.

"Opportunity is missed by most people because it is dressed in overalls and looks like work."

Thomas Edison

– 14 –

Do Better

contributed by Annette Barnard

Business was dismal. Competition was tough. Orders slowed. References led to dead ends.

I considered my assets. It wasn't my product—I offered the best. But my marketing department, well, it needed some help.

My name is Annette. It was 1962, and I was 12. My enterprise? Babysitting. Determined to rise to the top, I needed an edge.

Annette and her father, Walter A. Williamson

I went to my father. I had a thought. "Dad, can I use your typewriter?" I asked.

"Go for it," he said. "But make it great."

I typed away. A draft emerged. Not my best, but it would do. An advertisement of sorts. I'd plaster the neighborhood.

"Dad, can I use your mimeograph machine?" I asked. (This was before the days of printers.)

Again, my Dad complied. "Just make it shine," he said.

I printed out 20 copies and circled the neighborhood riding my bike. One for every mailbox in sight. Then I waited.

What happened? Nothing! My flyer flopped.

I went back to my father. "Dad," I cried, sad flyer in hand, "what should I do?"

Dad grabbed that paper out of my palm. He examined the remnant of my failed plan. Then guess what he said?

Two simple words. "Do better."

That's it. "Do better," said Dad.

I expected sympathy, perhaps a pat on the back. At least a "You did your best." I was ticked.

So, I stewed for a few days. But I couldn't stop thinking about those two simple words. Do better? I decided I'd show him. Do better? All right. That's what I'd do.

And I did. I thought extra hard. Then I had an idea.

The flyer became the *Canterbury Knight*, a newsletter named after our neighborhood. Contests and drawings. Local announcements. Snippets of neighborhood news. I even added a column of jokes.

The phones lit up. I was booked solid. I even raised rates. The *Canterbury Knight* saved my business. And the competition? I was too busy to care.

"Do better." The words of a man who walked what he talked.

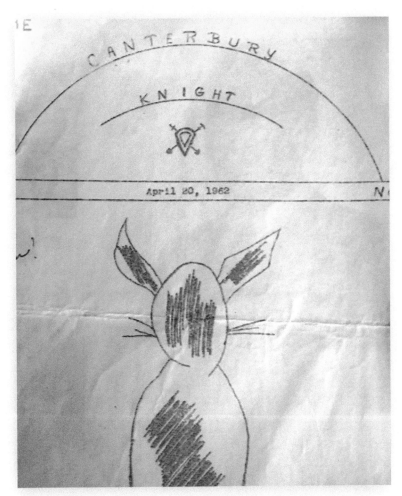

Original manuscript of one of the earliest editions of the *Canterbury Knight*

A survivor of the Depression, my dad was determined to rise. He did, big time. Dad became a self-made millionaire with no one to open doors, no formal training, and no college education.

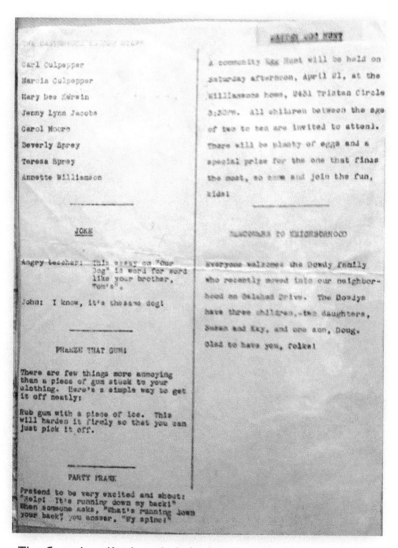

The *Canterbury Knight* included jokes, household tips, and community news

You know the exploding money that banks use to catch bank robbers? My Dad invented it. And the frozen popsicles kids love in summer? That was Dad too.

What did I learn from my dad? I never remember Dad sitting down to tell me I could do anything I wanted. Instead, he taught me how to make it happen, how to get it done. If things aren't working out, dig deeper, figure it out.

My father inspired me to be more than I would ever have been. I went from a high school dropout to commencement speaker at my university.

"Do better," Dad said. "You always can."

He was right.

Annette's dad, Walter, inspired her to "do better," and she spent her career continuing his legacy by helping others do better

ABOUT THE CONTRIBUTOR

Annette Barnard is a retired educator living in Scottsdale, Arizona. She dedicated her professional life to putting children in the best possible position to succeed academically, socially, and emotionally. Annette was a special education teacher, a regular education teacher, and an elementary school principal. She has a wonderful grown daughter, a great son-in-law, and two fabulous grandchildren. Annette is happily married and has earned many awards and acknowledgments in her life, but one of the most precious was the understanding that her Dad was proud of her.

*"No, no! The adventures first, explanations take
such a dreadful time."*

Lewis Carroll

− 15 −

Camping Adventures

contributed by Corey Hague

Summer of '88. Flagstaff, Arizona. My name is Corey. I was six. My brothers, Brian and Casey, were nine and five.

We begged and begged Dad, adventure this time! "Hunting," we said. "We're ready to die."

Older brother Brian carried the weapon of choice, a BB gun loaded with ammo and ready to go. He was also entrusted with our sack of dried peaches for fuel.

I sported a Rambo knife. Little brother Casey had plastic Chinese throwing stars and foam nunchucks affixed to his side. Dad carried my compass so we wouldn't get lost. Camouflage, bandanas, and black face paint; off we marched into the woods.

Dad strolled down the trail as we darted around. We crunched in the leaves and hid behind trees. It was a blast.

As we emerged from a ditch, I thought, "The trail's not there!" Dad sat on a stump, a few feet away.

"Dad, are we on the trail?" I was hoping for a yes.

"No, we're lost," he calmly said.

"Lost!" I exclaimed with concern. I wondered, do dads get lost?

Dad pulled out my compass. "Follow me," he waved with a smile. To the trail, I thought.

An hour went by. Dad suddenly stopped.

"The compass is broken!" he said with disgust.

I felt panic. "Dad, the compass is right. I use it a lot." But I wondered, was I right?

We walked for hours, then more. "Let's stop for a snack to recharge," Dad said. "Brian, dried peaches for all."

Brian looked sick. With a whimper he 'fessed up, "Sorry, I ate them at the last stop." (I think Dad already knew.)

"Too bad," Dad said. "The night without food." The night?! "This compass is wrong," Dad mumbled again.

Casey, Corey, and Brian Hague, ready for a camping adventure

"Dad!" I scolded, "I used that compass on the drive here. It worked then." I shouted at Brian, "It's your fault. You ate all the peaches. Now Dad's too weak to find the way home!"

Then they appeared.

Wolves, stone-still in the clear.

Dad snapped out of a spell, gathered us close, stepped up like a shield, picked up a stick, unsheathed my knife, and looked hard at those wolves with a don't-you-dare stare.

The wolves looked at Dad in a most curious way. In less than a minute they trotted away.

With understandable fear we looked up at Dad. "Time to go home," he casually said.

Within minutes the campsite appeared. How did Dad get there so fast? At that moment, we didn't care. But it did come up later at dinner. "Dad, how did we get back so fast?" I asked.

Dad smiled and said, "Corey, we were always just minutes away. You guys asked for adventure. That's what you got."

As it turns out, Dad walked us in circles. The compass was right.

Casey then asked, "But the wolves?"

Dad burst out laughing, "Now, *that* was a surprise."

I look back 25 years on that adventure with Dad. It meant a lot. He was always doing crazy, unexpected things. Those became the memories we sit around and laugh about today.

The Hague family 15 years later, still lost in the woods. From left: Cousin Jason, Casey, Corey, Greg, Roseann, and Brian

While I didn't realize it at the time, I learned a valuable lesson from the way Dad brought us up. He was demanding and firm when it came to grades, behavior and such. He expected a lot from my brothers and me (and still does). But Dad also made life incredibly fun.

I learned I could lead a life of lofty goals and dedication to accomplishment, while having a great time every step of the way.

ABOUT THE CONTRIBUTOR

Corbin Hague resides in Phoenix, Arizona. He co-owns and operates Flexground, a company specializing in rubberized playground surfacing for child safety.

"Peace is not the absence of conflict; it is the ability to handle conflict by peaceful means."

Ronald Reagan

– 16 –

Know When to Walk Away

contributed by Rudy Ruettiger

Notre Dame is a legendary place. A spot in the class means working your brain. A spot on the team means a chance at great fame.

But—bullied, badgered, and mad—I became a rebel in high school. Sophomore year it came to a head. I befriended a rough kid who well could have spelled my end.

A big fight was planned for that Friday night. My friend said, "Rudy, we're tough. Let's go."

I foolishly agreed. I had a big head. It was a chance to show off. I'd smear those kids who had made me so mad.

I waited until the family was fast asleep. Quietly, I slid out of bed, pulled on my clothes, and tiptoed to the back door. I was careful not to make a sound.

But Dad knew something was up. He cut me off at the door. With his hand on my shoulder, he insisted we talk.

I admitted where I was headed. The kids we would fight had belittled us. It was our turn to teach 'em some stuff.

That's when Dad rescued my future, and maybe my life. He replied, "You are no man when a meaningless fight is your way to prove it. You become a man by knowing when to walk away. Learn it now and remember."

I'm blessed that Dad stayed up to catch me that night. Bad news came the next day. Several were badly hurt in the fray. With a blow to the head, my friend was now dead.

It could have been me, or I might have been cuffed and taken away. Either way, that would have spelled the end of my dream—no Notre Dame.

Dad, you were the best. You taught me to stop the big talk, get in life's game, to go out and fight, to make the big plays. But you taught me one other critical thing.

To know when to walk away.

About the Contributor

Rudy Ruettiger, #45, is a legend himself. He made the Notre Dame class. He then went on to become the heart of the Fighting Irish—and have his story told in the acclaimed 1993 film, *Rudy*.

His dad, Daniel Ruettiger, was a war hero and legendary dad. Married a world-class mom. Had 14 kids. Worked three jobs. Yet he always found time to attend his kids' games.

Rudy quotes his father to show how his father's advice inspired his path in life, "Stop the talk and do the hard walk. If you want Notre Dame, you need to make better grades. If you intend to play in the game, you'd better get in the shape of your life. Don't tell me you will; come back and show me you did."

Rudy's dad, Daniel Ruettiger, in uniform

*"A truly strong person does not need the approval
of others any more than a lion needs
the approval of sheep."*

Vernon Howard

– 17 –

Shepherd or Sheep?

contributed by Katie Landon

My sophomore year in high school.

I forget what theatre. I forget what movie. But I will never forget what Dad did that day.

A group of people were standing in queue, waiting to buy tickets.

I instinctively looked for the back of the line and proceeded that way.

But Dad? He walked right around them!

I paused for a second, figuring he would see, come back, and join me in line. But Dad gave me a wave and marched on.

I reluctantly followed.

I could feel the scowls. The accusatory stares. Line standers glared at us with condemning eyes as we passed.

So embarrassing.

But when we got to the front, we discovered that the line was actually for a special screening of a new movie!

Dad and I walked right up to an available counter and bought tickets.

As we entered the theater, a manager came out and announced, "This line is for the special screening only. If you are seeing another movie, please proceed to the front to buy tickets."

Above: Katie and her dad, John, showing off creations from the Indian Princesses summer camp they attended together in Dallas.

Left: Katie and her dad on her 22nd birthday

Guess what? About half the people in that line scurried up to the front, grumbling about having to wait so long.

"Sheep," Dad chuckled under his breath as the entry attendant tore our tickets.

Sheep, I pondered?

As we waited for the movie to start, I asked Dad what he meant.

"Honey, most people live like sheep. They stay close to the flock. They like the security and comfort of groups. They gravitate to the back of the long lines.

"Many years ago, I decided to live my life as a shepherd, not as a sheep."

As the movie started, I looked around at the people sitting in rows.

Sheep? Was I one of them?

Driving home, the subject came up again.

"Ok," Dad said, "next week I want you to test the theory at school. Be first to your classroom after lunch, close the door, and simply stand there waiting to go in. See how many people line up behind you, just assuming that the door is locked."

The following Monday, I did just that.

I made it a point to arrive at my English classroom first after lunch. The door was already closed, but unlocked.

Let the experiment begin.

I stood outside, waiting for sheep.

The first student took her place in line behind me, without even asking or trying the door handle.

Then another.

And another.

Within minutes, a long line formed behind me, a flock of sheep.

No one asked. Nobody tried to open the door. They all just assumed.

Finally, the teacher arrived. At last, a shepherd to lead the sheep. She certainly knew the door was not locked.

But when she saw all of us standing there, she started fumbling for her keys to unlock the door! She then proceeded to insert and turn her key in the lock, only to discover that she had locked the door.

That day at the movie with Dad. A lesson I won't forget.

With all that I do—am I a shepherd, or am I a sheep?

ABOUT THE CONTRIBUTOR

Katie Landon was raised in Dallas, Texas, by her parents with her three siblings. She graduated from the University

of Arizona and recently moved to Scottsdale with Roxie, her Golden Retriever. Katie works as a second-grade teacher for the Scottsdale Unified School District.

Katie accepted a marriage proposal from her boyfriend, Adam, on July 26, 2013.

"If a man does not keep pace with his companions, perhaps it is because he hears a different drummer."

Henry David Thoreau

– 18 –

Junk Food Rap

contributed by Brian Hague

The announcement came over the school PA.

Every eye turned and focused squarely on me. What should I do? Run for the door? Slide under the desk? If embarrassment is fatal, I am now dead.

I knew right away. It was my dad. He was doing it again!

My name is Brian. It's been 23 years. I was 11. Monday morning. Fifth grade. Ms. Sullivan's class.

Two days before. Dad had taken my brothers and me to the swap meet. We were trolling the grounds for trick stuff.

Then, something caught Dad's eye. Actually, his ear. It was D. J. Carlos, a Latin rapper in hip-hop gear, selling personalized songs right out of his van.

The sign read, "Custom Rap Songs. You write it; I rap it."

Dad strolled over. I thought nothing of it.

But Monday morning, the loudspeaker blared.

"Kids!" the principal chirped. "Something special today!

"Junk Food Rap by the healthiest 40-year-old in Arizona, Brian Hague's dad!"

Heads whipped around. Kids pointed, some giggled, some laughed aloud. Then it began. A drum machine beat over the PA. DJ Carlos rapping in.

"Protein makes you grow, fat makes you slow, carbs make you go, junk food makes you say 'Whooooaaa!'" On and on it continued to play. (Dad has preached nutrition since I was a kid. He's into that.)

I buried my head in my hands in embarrassment. This was torture of Brian, orchestrated by Dad.

But then, I glanced up.

What?

Brian, as a kid, with his savvy dad, Greg Hague

My friends were tapping their feet! It was a pretty cool beat.

Attitudes changed. All of a sudden, my classmates were into the scene. I was a celebrity. My dad was a hit.

Who would have thunk? Nutrition by rap.

I learned something important that day. My dad taught me the value of finding a different, better way to approach life. Don't be afraid. As they say, get outside the box.

Want to make an impression? Find a cool way.

ABOUT THE CONTRIBUTOR

Brian Hague, now 34, lives in San Diego. He is the oldest son of Greg Hague. Father and son work together to share stories of remarkable dads at www.*savvydad.com*. Brian is also an accomplished musician. Check out Brian's hit video "Go Gettas" on YouTube and his other music at *reverbnation.com/trigs*.

> *"I hold that a strongly marked personality can influence descendants for generations."*
>
> Beatrix Potter

– 19 –

In His Corner

contributed by John Hite

With hunting season underway, it wasn't the sight of three men with rifles that made me uneasy. It was their demeanor.

I watched as the trio flagged down my buddy's truck on the dusty dirt road twenty yards ahead. I couldn't make out the words, but the message was clear.

Tommy Hite and sons in 1988: Richard, Steven, John (at top), David, and Dad, Tommy

Arms flailing. One spat in the road. Go home. Get out of here.

I quickly put my truck in park and slid out. "Son," I said to my six-year-old boy, "stay here." I approached the three angry men. "What's the problem?"

"This is our land. Ya'll are hunting where you don't belong," said the man in blue flannel. He was clearly the ringleader. "Think it's time for you and your people to get out."

"This is my dad's land, and I'm not going anywhere," I shot back. I knew damned well the boundaries of the Hite land.

My family had been here for nine generations. These men were the trespassers, not us.

The argument became heated, the situation quickly escalating out of control. The guy in the other truck hurriedly radioed the sheriff.

A 1982 shot of John Hite and his family: David, Richard, Carolyn, baby Steven, Tommy, and John

My dad, Tommy, heard the call on his CB radio. He was first to the scene.

Father's truck screeched to a halt. A former college athlete, he was an imposing man, 6'2" and broad-shouldered. I knew Dad had never been afraid to make a stand for what's right.

"What are you doing on MY land?" he challenged the men. "Intimidating my son and grandson? You want to mess with someone? Try messing with me."

As quickly as it all had escalated, it fizzled. The strangers grumbled and left. I was, once again, in awe of my dad.

My father had a way of taking control. At home. With others. No matter how bad things were. Dad could step in and defuse any situation. And, as his son, I knew I could count on Dad to be at my side.

This is only one "Tommy story" I could relay. My dad, a father of four sons, was always in his boys' corner.

The Hite family in 2011: Steven, David, Tommy, Carolyn, Richard, and John

He was quick to tell us when we were wrong. He would firmly straighten us out. But we knew he would always be there for us. He was 100% in our corner, no matter what.

It's like having the biggest kid in the playground on your side, always. Gives you confidence. As I grew older I learned that confidence in kids endures for life.

Today, with four children of my own, I intend to stay in my kids' corner as well as my dad's. I want to be there for him like he was for me.

About the Contributor

At just 20 years old, a mere sophomore in college, John Hite showed the confidence his dad had inspired. He had the guts to "go for it."

On a shoestring budget, with a very small loan co-signed by Dad, John, and a childhood friend founded a company. It was a harebrained idea to most. But as you could guess, Dad encouraged, helped and advised from day one.

The company, then College Comfort, rented cushioned stadium seats to college sports fans. It started at Virginia Tech, John's alma mater, and today serves over 130 colleges.

John and his partner eventually sold College Comfort to ISP Sports. It was then acquired by IMG World (founded in 1960 by golf legend Arnold Palmer and Mark McCormack). John stayed on and works there to this day as VP.

Despite his financial success, John lives within three miles of his parents, as do his brothers.

> *"It is our choices that show what we truly are, far more than our abilities."*
>
> Harry Potter and the Chamber of Secrets

– 19 –

Goofus

contributed by Naomi Reed Rhode

Goofus he was, a penguin indeed. The most beautiful bird I'd ever seen. The curve of his wooden wings. The carved grooves in his beak. Dad's gift to me.

Summer camp, just one week away. Not just any camp. A co-ed retreat, a camp with the boys. I was giddy. Nervous.

"Co-ed," I said, as it spread to my friends. A signal to all. Naomi is becoming a very big girl. I was just 12, going on 20. Prepared for adventure. (Ready for love?)

Dad, a Methodist pastor, had shown the way. His deeds were strong. I heeded his words. My father knew this was real big. He trusted. But Dad wasn't dumb. Things can happen at camp, even one sponsored by church.

"Naomi," he said, pressing Goofus into the flesh of my hand, "This is a special gift. I carved it for you. It's to take with you to camp. Everywhere, in fact."

A penguin, I thought, lovely for sure, but … "Thank you, Daddy. Why?"

My father replied, "Naomi, you're an amazing young lady. Smart as a whip. A future so big. This little guy? So you'll never forget."

That's all he said. I knew what he meant.

Naomi and her father, Virgil, wilderness camping

Goofus and I packed up for camp.

It was a marvelous time. I came home eager to tell. "And Goofus?" asked Dad.

"Well, I gave him away!" I excitedly said. "I met a boy. I fell in love! Goofus was my gift to him."

What a shock that must have been for Dad. But he was unshaken. Dad's exact words? (Preserved in my little red diary.)

"He must be a phenomenal man, Naomi. Because you always make good choices. And you always make your choices good, too."

What happened next? You'll never guess.

Seven years passed. I married that man.

It's 56 years later. We're still married today.

Why? That powerful lesson from Dad.

Jim and I made a choice way back then. We also made a decision to make that choice good.

What did I learn from Dad and Goofus?

Make choices. Make them good.

About the Contributor

Naomi Reed Rhode's husband, Jim, carried Goofus with him for years, until one sad day Goofus was lost with their luggage in flight. Goofus is gone, but his memory lives on. Remember, Naomi still has Jim on her arm.

Naomi's father, Virgil Asbury Reed, passed when she was 13. His lessons would last a lifetime. She writes about them in *My Father's Hand: A Daughter's Reflections on A Father's Wisdom.*

Jim and Naomi today

"Faith is the strength by which a shattered world shall emerge into the light."

Helen Keller

– 21 –

High Ground

contributed by Justin Hyde

At the Hyde household, love was abundant; resources were few.

What we ate for dinner had often roamed the forest that day. Neighbors were miles apart. As a boy, I longed to hunt with Dad. I pleaded but was told, "Justin, you're too young."

But the day finally came. I was six. Dad carried my gun - the sling was too big for my tiny shoulder. We started the trek up the mountain. It seemed like we walked forever. Father and son moved quietly through the brush. We didn't want to frighten the prey. Shadows grew long. Darkness began to fall.

Finally, Dad found our spot. We crouched in the brush. We waited. Our breath. The rustle of trees. No other sound.

Suddenly, an elk jumped out and shot into the brush. Dad quickly leapt up. "Don't move from this spot," he ordered. In a flash, my father was gone.

I was alone. I tried to be brave. Seconds, then minutes, passed. My breath quickened, and panic set in. What if something happened to Dad? What would happen to me?

"Dad," I whispered, then again, and then louder once more.

Tears streamed down my cheeks. Finally I cried out, "DAD, PLEASE HELP ME! Where are you?"

Suddenly, from behind a tree a few feet away, my father appeared.

"Justin, I've been here the whole time. I would never on purpose leave you alone. Catch your breath, calm down. I did this for a reason. Now, tell me, which way is our home?"

We had walked for miles. I couldn't say. In the dim light, I saw only trees. My father gently grasped my small

Justin's dad, Kevin Hyde

hand. We then climbed up through the woods and reached the high ground. He said, "Justin, if anything ever happens to Dad, walk to high ground."

Dad then pointed to a faint glow in the darkness below, "See the light? That's our home."

"Your Dad's not always going to be around, Justin. When you feel scared or alone, when you don't know what to do, find the high ground. And, remember, there's something bigger looking out for you."

I nodded. I understood.

Together, we knelt to the ground. We prayed—for our family, our home, the woods, and the creatures that roamed. We thanked God for giving us each other, this wonderful life, for helping us find the high ground, and helping us know the way home.

ABOUT THE CONTRIBUTOR

Justin Hyde is a father himself. At just over 30, Justin has already achieved great success. He is co-founder of The Hyde-Norton Group, a worldwide strategic planning and risk management firm. He also owns interests in auto dealerships, health clubs, resorts, ranches, hotels, biotechnology firms and the Utah Blaze pro football team.

Justin co-founded the annual Rocky Mountain Economic Summit & Retreat, an invitation-only event covered live by Bloomberg TV, CNBC, and Reuters.

Justin served on Mitt Romney's 2012 Finance Team as the Wyoming State Finance Chair and is a leader in the Boy Scouts.

Justin Hyde (right) and Dad, Kevin, (third from right) with family and friends

"The bad boy: Always more fun."

Ian McShane

– 22 –

Johnny Be Bad

contributed by Chris Haydel

"Stay away from that Johnny—he's trouble," Mom warned. "He's a troublemaker, a bad seed." As a nurse, Mom had observed the sometimes tragic result of hanging out with "dangerous" kids.

It was a hot summer day in New Orleans, but to me, it had never felt cooler.

I had saved up for a month, and today was the big day.

The shiny long barrel. The plastic "ivory" grip. Multi-cap loading capacity.

A magnificent weapon. A young boy's dream.

I had seen it in the toy aisle of a store not too far away.

Mom had gone out to run errands, but she promised to take me as soon as she got back. I was playing outside to kill time.

Johnny was outside too, but he was killing bugs with his magnifying glass. "Hey, watcha doin'?" He yelled from

The Haydel family, Christmas 1971

across the street. "Nothing," I mumbled, bowing my head, heeding Mom's warning.

I shuffled my feet for a minute and looked up. Johnny was now standing on the lawn, just a few feet away. Glaring at me with mischievous eyes, he was clearly sizing me up. Not good, I thought.

"I'm just waiting for my mom to take me to the mall to buy a new cap gun," I said as I shuffled my feet, staring down at the ground. I was really hoping he would take the hint and get lost.

But before he opened his mouth, I realized I had disclosed too much.

"You don't need to wait for your Mommy... c'mon, let's go," he sneered, tugging at my shirt. "You'll have the gun and be back before your mom even gets home."

I should've said no. I knew it for sure. Should've just plopped right down on the lawn in protest. But at 11 years old, a boy's pride, so wanting to be "cool," it blinded my mind to good sense, to doing what I knew I shouldn't do. So I went.

As we arrived at the first street corner, the first red flag went up. Or thumb, I should say. It was Johnny's thumb! Apparently, we were hitchhiking to the mall!

Before I knew it, Johnny flagged down a car. He climbed in. Stupidly, so did I. Neither of us knew the driver. Within minutes, we were swept away from the safety of our neighborhood.

I was scared. But I also felt a sense of excitement different and more intense than I had ever felt before. Just "bad boy" Johnny and me. Hitching a ride to buy guns. Rebels on the loose!

Is this what being bad feels like? It was a fascinating thought.

Chris Haydel (far right) with his dad and his sister, Cheryl, at a family celebration

Well, lucky for me, the worst didn't occur. Had that been the case, I might not be here today. Our "chauffeur" was a nice guy and dropped us off in front in the mall. We raced each other into the building, straight to the toy aisle.

There it was, more beautiful than I remembered it. But something else I hadn't remembered. It didn't come with caps, and I only had enough money for the gun.

And what good is a gun with no ammo? Johnny detected his cue. "Go buy the gun," he whispered, "then come back and meet me here when you're done."

I knew his intent, and I protested at first. Hitchhiking was one thing—stealing was something else. But again, I went with the flow. I was getting in deep. The curse of being "cool" had consumed me. I couldn't say no.

In a zombie-like trance, I went to the front, bought the gun, and reported back to Johnny in the aisle. He revealed a handful of caps he had tucked close to his chest.

"Here, put 'em in the bag," he slithered in a most devious tone.

For a split second, I snapped out of it, "No!" I hissed back.

"Fine, then I'll do it!" he snarled, grabbing for the bag. I clutched my bag tight, and in a reaction of intense haste and frustration, I angrily swiped the extra caps from his hand and thrust them in the bag!

Then it happened. Adventure turned bad. It felt like a great white shark latching down on my left arm with a force that spun me around. "What do ya think yer doing?" he growled, his breath hot and putrid in my face.

The shiny brass buttons of his security uniform streaked through my vision as he shook the bag loose from my grasp. He had us both by our scrawny little arms, one in each hand.

A massive man. A weathered, militant face. My eyes immediately welled up. Johnny was defiant, stone cold. He didn't flinch an inch.

We were both dragged to the back, through the "Employees Only" door. It was grey and bleak—quite the contrast from the colorful toy aisle just seconds before.

I was so scared, my brain was virtually paralyzed.

I don't even remember being put in the holding cell, but that's where we ended up.

I was sobbing. Sniffling. Sick to my stomach.

A criminal behind bars.

And Johnny? Not a single tear. Not one sign of remorse. After a while, they let me out and cuffed me to a chair while a lady asked me questions and typed up my responses for the report. "So why did you come with him?" she asked, her eyes gesturing disapprovingly toward Johnny. At that point I realized … everyone did know Johnny.

Back in the cell, Johnny laughed, saying, "Yeah, I got busted stealing here once before, and my dad busted my tooth over it, see?" As he pulled down his lip to reveal the broken tooth, my stomach dropped and my heart broke, simultaneously.

Would his dad hit him again? Would my dad hit me? Bust my tooth?

My dad was the kindest, funniest, most gentle guy in the world. We always played word games in the car together. A beloved pediatrician in the community. Always upbeat.

My father was the man I respected most. But hitchhiking? Stealing? I feared for my life—and my teeth.

After what felt like a whole day in that cell, the security guard finally came for me.

"Good luck! Hope it doesn't hurt too bad!" Johnny snorted on my way out.

I was taken to a separate office. Dad was already standing there, arms folded, furrowed brow.

Eyes closed and head down, I began weeping uncontrollably. My life was over.

In just one day, I had ruined everything. He would never love me again. Never respect me again. I was devastated. And then I felt his arms wrap around me.

He didn't say a word. He just hugged me until I stopped crying.

We drove home in silence, a major deviation from our normal word play.

Days went by. Dad didn't speak to me at all. Not a word. At breakfast. At dinner. Before bed. Utter silence.

I did extra chores. Extra homework. Extra anything I could think of to start winning back his respect. I missed him so much. I missed our conversations, our word games, just having him in my life.

After two weeks, I could take no more. The silence was unbearable.

I approached him, "Dad, can you please just tell me what my punishment is so I can do it and we can go back to normal?" He motioned for me to sit down.

"Son, you've given yourself more punishment in the past two weeks than I ever could have." I blinked, bewildered by the response.

He continued, "Why do you think I play word games with you all the time?"

"To help my vocabulary," I said, remembering what he had told me.

"Yes, that's true, but more importantly, it's to teach you to think ... before you speak, before you act, before you do anything. The worst situations in life usually start as rash, foolish, impulsive, seemingly small, but bad decisions."

Dad continued, "I wanted to give you time to think about that."

Dad was a man of infinite patience. He also knew how to mentor, teach, and make a message stick.

My mom was loving, but in a different way. If she had picked me up from "jail" that day, I may have gotten that busted tooth after all!

Thanks, Dad. My life is so much better because of you.

ABOUT THE CONTRIBUTOR

Chris Haydel lives in Pasadena, California, where he strives to bring the wisdom and compassion of his father to the life he shares with his wife, Pilar, and son, Santiago. He is the founder and president of Haydel, Biel & Associates, a registered investment advisory firm. Chris's passion for investment knowledge is matched only by his love of music, especially the music of his hometown, New Orleans. Whenever possible, you will find him promoting, cultivating or assisting the music and musicians of the Crescent City—maybe coming soon to a town near you.

"The redeeming things in life are not happiness and pleasure but the deeper satisfactions that come out of struggle."

F. Scott Fitzgerald

– 23 –

Lesson by Contrast

contributed by Michael LeBoeuf

In many ways my father was a very good family man. He and my mother were married almost 63 years. He was faithful to my mother and brought home every penny he earned.

He was honest, did not drink nor gamble, and kept us out of debt. We always had a roof over our heads and food to eat, despite the fact that he had only an eighth-grade education.

However, in other ways my father had his shortcomings. He was a salesman who jumped from job to job, never staying with anything long enough to be successful.

The idea of having a plan and the self-discipline to stick with it was totally off of his radar. We always lived in rental housing except for a six-month period when I was three years old.

Michael's only photo of his father, Maurice, approximately 1970

My father built a house during World War II and sold it shortly after. Between my fourth and sixth birthdays, we lived in nine different residences in four different cities, ranging from Virginia to Texas.

When I was in high school and spent money on something he would tell me, "A fool and his money are soon parted." Ironically, he and my mother spent the last 20 years of their lives living on one Social Security check.

Whenever my sister or I asked why we seemed to have less money than other families, the excuse was always the same: It took everything he earned to provide for my sister and me. We were often reminded of what a struggle it is to have a family.

When the day came for my parents to drive me to college for my freshman year, my father had a temper tantrum and refused to take me. My aunt bailed me out and she and my mother brought me.

My mother didn't drive and neither did I. One way my father controlled the family was by being the only driver. As a result, my older sister and I did not drive until we were in our twenties.

In his late fifties, I heard him say, "I need to think about putting money away for retirement." I was in my mid-twenties and thought, "This poor guy doesn't have a clue."

Years later when I was a university professor and told him I was going to write a book he said, "You aren't planning to make any money with that book, are you?" I dedicated my first book to my parents. He told me he didn't read it, nor did he read any of the others I wrote after that.

When I was in grad school, someone told me about a visit she had with my father. She said that all he talked about was how well I was doing. He was clearly very proud, but the news came as a shock to me.

He finally did tell me that he was proud of me when he was 84 and I was 51. It was great to hear, but it would have meant a lot more if I had heard it much earlier in life.

My mother, on the other hand, was a saint. She believed in me, protected, encouraged, and supported me. She read every page of every book I wrote while she was alive. She was a very bright woman with whom I could communicate.

My mother was a homemaker but got a job so I could go to college and focus on studying without having to worry about working. Thanks to her I was able to go through undergrad school debt-free.

Michael's mother, "Vin," in 1972

While my mother was very willing to work so I could go away to college, she was no pushover. She made it very clear that this was a one-time offer. If I ever quit college and then decided I wanted to go back, it would be up to me to pay for it.

She put it this way, "You can study hard now, get a good education, and have a great life—or be like us and struggle for the rest of your life."

Shortly before I left for college she gave me a cartoon drawing of a farmer watching a dog who is in hot pursuit of a rabbit. The farmer asked, "Rabbit, are you gonna make it?" The rabbit replied, "Make it? I gotta make it!" The message to me was clear. I was the rabbit and made it my business to graduate.

I financed graduate school with summer jobs, student loans and an assistantship. I was determined to never live the kind of life my father lived.

My mother never said anything but I suspect she was thinking the same thing. When I walked across the graduation stage for the final time to get my PhD, I thought to myself, "Thanks, Mom. Your boy is going to be just fine."

Sometimes fathers leave us a gift by teaching us what not to do when we become parents. I would encourage every father to reflect back on his own dad's strengths and shortcomings.

Michael and his wife, Elke, in 2013

Resolve to practice and improve on the positives and stay away from the negatives as much as possible. A wise person learns from example and contrast.

As for my personal story, the most important message I leave with you with is this:

Be careful what you tell your children about how tough it is to be a parent if you ever hope to someday have grandchildren. Children who get the message that kids are a burden are more likely to opt out of becoming moms and dads. I chose to be childless, and my sister had only one child, who was likely unplanned. I suspect the messages we received as children had a lot to do with that.

And one final thought: financial support is important but emotional support is critical. Your children may forget what you say or do, but they will never forget how you made them feel.

Good luck, Savvy Dads. You have one of the two most important jobs in the world.

ABOUT THE CONTRIBUTOR

For 20 years, Michael LeBoeuf was Professor of Management at the University of New Orleans, retiring as Professor Emeritus at age 47 in 1989. He is currently a bestselling author and national speaker. His books have sold almost two million copies worldwide.

*"Success consists of getting up
just one more time than you fall."*

Oliver Goldsmith

– 24 –

Steps Down the Road

contributed by Alex Sortino

Dad ripped the sheets back from my body. It was too early. I was ticked.

"You're going to the tryouts," he commanded. There would be no debate.

I was 12, and obsessed with baseball (still am). I dreamed of playing professionally. The Flames were holding tryouts that day. This was a boys' traveling team, one of the best.

The traveling teams were the way to stay sharp in the little league offseason. They were all tough to make. The Flames were among the best.

I had cold feet. I'd tried before, but always got cut. What was the point? Cozy and warm seemed a much better choice.

But Dad dragged me out of bed, made sure I showered and ate. He saw me off to the tryouts that day. What happened? I got cut once again.

I was pretty down on myself. As hard as I tried, the other kids always seemed better. I told Dad that baseball was out of my life.

Now, as I look back, that was a big moment for me. It changed my perspective on failure. With his hand on my shoulder, the man I adored said something like this,

"Alex, in life, big wins often require small falls. Those are just steps down the road. Time after time, you've got to get in the game. You can't win if you don't show up and give it your all.

"When you look back, you'll sorely regret the mornings you stayed warm in that bed. You'll never know if those were wins that might have been.

"Take comfort in this. If you never win one single time, you can be proud you stayed in the game and continued to try."

Alex, a future baseball GM, with his dad, Dan, and younger brother

My name is Alex Sortino. I'm in college (Arizona State University). Thanks to that advice from my dad, I bounce out of the sack, keep my ego in check, forget

"These days I get out of bed early"

about pride and don't worry about falls.

It's paying off. I earned a hard-to-get, coveted spot as a marketing intern at the Peoria Sports Complex, spring training headquarters of the San Diego Padres and Seattle Mariners. I intend to become General Manager of a pro team.

It will happen, just wait and see. I don't care how many times I fall on my face. I no longer get stressed about a no. I learned that from Dad.

Those are just steps down the road.

Alex and his father are both huge Dallas Cowboys fans

ABOUT THE CONTRIBUTOR

Alex Sortino studied business administration at Arizona State University, is focused on a career in sports, and landed  a sought-after position as a marketing intern at the Peoria Sports Complex in Phoenix, Arizona. His dream job is becoming the General Manager for a major league baseball team.

– 25 –

Chicago Bears Time

contributed by Christopher Neck

My young daughter's soccer team and the Chicago Bears— what do they have in common? My daughter wanted to know.

"Dad," said GiGe, "soccer practice starts at 3:00. When mom takes me, we get there on time. When you take me, we get there at 2:40. Why?"

"Mom's on the clock most people use," I said. "Me—I'm on Chicago Bears time."

Tommy Neck played cornerback and safety for the Chicago Bears—and learned lessons that he passed on to his children and grandchildren

GiGe knew her grandpa, my dad, had played for the Bears. And he was a star. Tommy Neck. Cornerback and safety.

Tommy Neck, back in the day

1962. His rookie year. Practice. The first day. A goal for most athletes, a dream for most men.

Practice was scheduled for 2:00 on the dot. Dad was nervous but ready to rock. He thought, whatever it takes to wow the great coach, the legendary George Halas, "Papa Bear."

He stepped onto the field at 1:55. To his surprise, the team was already there, hitting, running, tackling, mixing it up.

"Son, you're late," Coach Halas boomed to my dad. Clearly Coach called this one wrong, Dad thought.

"No sir, I'm five minutes early. Practice starts at 2:00," Dad respectfully said.

Coach Halas grabbed my father by the jersey and yanked him aside.

"When you play for Chicago, you're on Bears time. When a meeting starts at 2:00, you're there at 1:40. When a practice starts at 6:00, you're ready to hit it at 5:40. Got it, Neck?"

"Yes, sir," Dad quickly said.

Coach Halas wasn't convinced. "Don't walk. Don't stop. Don't stand still for a second. You'll run this entire practice so you'll never forget."

Dad never forgot. When he told me, neither did I.

Back to my daughter. She wanted to know, "Twenty minutes early, why so important?"

My lesson to GiGe as passed down from Granddad?

Want to finish first? Show up early.

Arrive on time and you start from behind.

ABOUT THE CONTRIBUTOR

Christopher Neck, PhD, has been teaching college students for over 20 years. He is currently an Associate Professor of Management and University Master Teacher at Arizona State University. He is the author of six books and speaks to companies nationwide.

Then and now: Christopher Neck as the youngest member of Tommy Neck's family, and as the father of his own daughter and son, GiGe and Bryton

*"We can't help everyone,
but everyone can help someone."*

Ronald Reagan

– 26 –

Good Hearts,
Great Starts

contributed by Rita Davenport

Daddy taught me by example that what goes around comes around.

As a mechanic, he never passed a motorist with car trouble that he didn't pull over and try to help. Sometimes,

as a smart-mouthed teen-ager concerned about being late, I'd complain, "Do you have to stop and help everybody in the free world with the hood up on their car?"

He'd say, "Yes, little lady, I do, 'cause someday

James Miller McWhorter (also known as "Mr. Mac") was proud to give his "little lady," Rita, away on her wedding day

129

my babies may be out on a highway, and someone will stop and help them 'cause I stopped and helped this feller right now."

I've been out on a highway before and had car trouble. The folks Daddy stopped to help were nowhere around. But somebody did always stop and help.

I'd whisper to myself, "Thank you, Daddy!"

About the Contributor

Rita Davenport is an award-winning keynote speaker, seminar leader, humorist and author. She is an Arizona Woman of the Year and served as Arbonne International President for 20 years. Most proudly, she is a wife, mom, and Nana to granddaughters Reese and Claire Ray.

*"The most profound statements
are often said in silence."*

Lynn Johnston

– 27 –

When Silence Says More

contributed by Lee R. Crist

Winter of '48. Hollidaysburg, Pennsylvania. Snow was a part of everyday life.

My father, Charles Crist, was a fireman for the Pennsylvania Railroad. As a railroad employee, he was entitled to a "free pass" to anywhere on the "system."

Over New Years, Mom and Dad decided to take advantage of the free ride. They caught a train to Baltimore to visit my older sister.

I had turned 16 the August before and was a proud licensed driver. My family's only form of transportation was a royal blue 1936 Ford Coupe with a rumble seat.

Catherine and Charles Crist

A proud, newly-licensed Lee Crist

Just before he left, my Dad instructed, "If it snows, leave the car in the garage."

Off they went. I had the car to myself. My buddies and I were going to have a blast!

The next morning, wouldn't you know, I woke up to six inches of snow. There were very few snowplows in those days, so the roads stayed covered in white.

I had a decision to make ... follow my father's instructions or take a chance and hope I would never get caught.

I picked up three of my buddies. One sat up front. Two in the rumble seat.

We drove to the next town where the girls lived, slipping and sliding all the way.

Coming back later that day, the right front wheel suddenly slid off the road. We took out a mailbox and landed against a tree. We were shaken, not hurt.

The car was another story.

We'd hit the tree dead center. The bumper, grill, radiator, distributor, and water pump were toast!

What was I going to do? My dad would kill me, or worse.

One of my buddies, Pody Waters, said he had a buddy who would tow us to his uncle's welding shop.

When Pody's uncle saw that beat-up car, he just shook his head.

I called my Uncle How'd and told him what happened. He said, "Whatever you do, you better get it done before your dad gets home. He's NOT going to be happy."

We toiled for two days with Pody's uncle. We used a torch. It only got worse.

It was the eve of day two. We were still trying to put "Humpty Dumpty back together again."

Suddenly, the old wooden garage door slowly opened, and there stood Dad.

I was petrified. What would he do? A lickin' was coming. I would be grounded for life.

Dad said not a word.

He slowly walked around the car, stood still for a moment, looked up, and paused.

With a look of disappointment, he quietly said, "I told you to let the car in the garage if it snowed."

He turned and walked out.

I felt sick. My heart sank. I had betrayed my dad's trust.

To his dying day, my father never mentioned that car again.

And to this day, I've never forgotten my dad's silence or look of disappointment. It's made a difference in how I've lived my life.

About the Contributor

Lee Crist is a retired sales executive, one heck of a golfer, and the best father-in-law a guy could ask for. He lives in Duncansville, Pennsylvania, with his bride of 57 years, Barbara.

Lee and Barb Crist with their daughters, Terrie, Bobbie, and Roseann

Lee and Barb Crist with their four children and the "Grands"

*"Son, something special happened today.
We just became friends."*

Harold Hague

– 28 –

Dad and Me . . .
Taking a Pee
by Greg Hague

You're the first. No one else knows. Too embarrassing. Please keep it down.

It's about Chubby. And me. Taking a pee.

I was 15. I wanted to fly. On a small grass airstrip close to our home, the owner gave lessons in a beat up Cessna 150. I had asked Chubby if I could learn to fly. He said, "Way too young."

I couldn't resist. I did it anyway.

I rode my bike to the airport each Saturday. My grass cutting earnings covered a lesson each week. I came to love flying like nothing else in my life. Still do.

The day finally came when my instructor stepped out of the plane. This was my solo. So proud, I had to tell Dad. I figured he would be furious. Still, I couldn't resist. (I had a "resistance" problem, even back then.)

At dinner that night, I confessed, "Dad, I'm sorry, I know you said no, but I went ahead. I've been taking flying lessons. I went up alone, I flew solo today. I know you're going to be mad. But Dad, I'm so excited, and proud, and happy, I just wanted you to know."

Absolute silence. Two, maybe three minutes went by. A storm had to be brewing. This was gonna be bad.

Then Chubby quietly said, "Greg, tomorrow I want to meet your instructor. Now go to bed."

I headed upstairs. That was it? I was seriously worried. This was so weird. What would he do? What would he say to my instructor the next day?

So what happened? Chubby had flown in WWII. In a nutshell, he met Moose, my instructor, took a few lessons, renewed his license, and got back up in the air.

Moose, my flight instructor

Chubby paid for the rest of my training, so it went pretty fast. We rented a plane and took off on our first flight, father and son. I knew this would be great.

Off we flew. It was unimaginably exciting, except for one thing. We didn't consider the issue of having to pee.

The wind kicked up. I was a brand new pilot, not skilled enough to land in bad weather. Chubby's skills were rusty too. We couldn't set down. We were stuck in the air.

Things got bad. We both really had "to go." I'm talking real pain. Today, we have "piddle packs" for small plane guys. (There's a different version for ladies—imagine that.) But, back then we had to squeeze tight and hold on, or drench the seat and the floor. That was no option with Dad sitting in the seat beside me. I'm sure he felt the same way.

Desperation can make people do dangerous things. Live or die, we finally decided to land that plane.

Dad purchased his first airplane in 1970

Chubby was in the left seat. He was the pilot. It wasn't pretty, but Dad got us down. We scrambled out the doors, father and son standing next to the wing, letting 'er roar. The sighs of relief were something to behold.

Then came the moment I remember to this day. Dad turned and said, "Son, something special happened today. We just became friends."

I felt like I had just come of age. My dad was my friend.

Dad was right. From that day forward, we were best friends. Chubby and I flew, motorcycled, helped each

other, and worked together for the rest of his life.

I learned a valuable lesson from that day in the air, the pain, the fear, and the lifelong bond I established with my father.

Parents and kids can be more than family—they can be friends.

Chubby loved to fly

"Clear eyes. Full hearts. Can't lose."

Coach Taylor, *Friday Night Lights*

– 29 –

Don't Act Special

contributed by Shane Beamer

Growing up the son of a football coach, I realized quickly that the profession is full of highs and lows. This was true for me, as well as my dad. I was as good as Dad's last game. When Dad won, he was smart. Lose, and he was a bum. Hero or culprit—week after week, it also identified me.

Coach Frank Beamer

There's so much attention given to college football. The results of Saturday games are magnified every week. This affects not only the team and coaches, but their families as well. Wherever you go, fans are quick to point out what they think of your dad.

In Hokie Nation, Frank Beamer is king. He coaches Virginia Tech's legendary football team.

While some of his peers have struggled with controversy, my dad is an example of doing it right. He turns out winners in sports, winners in class, and winners *with* class. Thanks in part to his leadership, Virginia Tech's academic rankings and ethical reputation are among the best in the world.

I have always watched my dad in the spotlight and under pressure. Two things really stand out:

1. Don't act special. Too many times "celebrities" are put on pedestals and act entitled. They expect to be treated a certain way. Not my dad. Never once did I see him act like he deserved to be treated differently than the next guy. He's never turned down an autograph or picture with a fan.

2. Stay even-keeled. This profession is full of peaks and valleys. If you're riding an emotional roller coaster day to day, good luck surviving. Win or lose, Dad is always the same even-tempered guy the next day. His teams play that way, too.

My dad is the same humble, appreciative, wonderful person today that he was in 1992. That was the year his team won only two games and he almost got fired. He hasn't changed. Whether in athletics or life, I try to live the same way.

No matter your fame, be kind and stay sane. Level heads make winning plays.

ABOUT THE CONTRIBUTOR

Since 2011, Shane Beamer has been at his dad's side as Associate Head Coach. Like his dad, Shane forged his career first as an outstanding player, then as a coach.

*"I won't cry, I won't cry, no, I won't shed a tear,
just as long as you stand, stand by me ...."*
Ben E. King

– 30 –

I'll Do It Too

contributed by Lora Jarocki.

Big, burly and bearded, Rocky was a biker; tough as a nail. He was my dad - and a pretty good "housewife," too.

We lived in Mountain Home, Idaho, a very small town. Mom, a Civil Engineer with the Air Force, traveled for work. With her away so much, Dad raised my sister and me.

When I was nine, Mom was assigned to South Korea. She would be gone a whole year.

Dad said, "You and I are the grownups now." Together, we would take care of my little sis', the house and ourselves.

All was so good. Then the lice came to town. "Epidemic," they said.

I awoke one morning and went off to school. At a stop in the ladies room, I ran my fingers through my hair. Unless you've had lice in your scalp, you can't know what it felt like. I screamed with disgust, shock and fear. I ran to see the school nurse.

The lice were so bad she ordered me home. I was instructed to wait outside for a ride. Sitting on the school steps, I felt like a freak, cast out and alone. I started to cry.

Dad soon arrived, gave me a hug and said "Lora, don't worry, I know what to do."

Together, for days, we tried it all. Dad spent over $100 on medicinal shampoos. We laundered the linens, towels, and clothes in our home. In desperation, Dad fired up the vacuum and ran the attachment through my hair. The shampoos were useless. The vacuum clogged up. Our clothes re-infested.

Finally, with a sorrowful face, Dad sat me down in the kitchen.

"Lora," he said, hand on my knee, "we have to do something you're not going to like."

From behind his back he produced a pair of electric black clippers. "Honey, we have no choice." I knew he was right. Dad slipped a towel on my shoulders. The clippers started to hum. My eyes quickly watered with tears.

I gazed up at my biker tough dad. Swollen red eyes. Streaming wet face. I could see his heart cried similar

Lora and Rocky Jarocki faced a close shave—together

tears. Before it ended, a torrent of daughter-dad tears and swatches of hair rained down on the floor.

"Now," Dad said, turning to me, "my turn."

He took my exact place on that same kitchen chair, fired up the clippers and plunged into his own mass of hair. I helped in the back and clipped close to his ears. Together, we walked over and looked in the mirror. I marveled at Dad's shiny bald head glowing with mine. Our eyes had now dried. We looked at each other and shrugged, grinned, then we hugged.

My hair, of course, would eventually grow back. But it wasn't the last I'd see of the clippers.

Every fall for twelve straight years, Dad ceremoniously shaved his head bald. "Penance," he said, though I assured him there was nothing to forgive.

I've faced some tough times since that day in my life.

What got me through? The memory of that grinning big guy in the mirror standing by me—my tough biker dad, head shiny and bald.

ABOUT THE CONTRIBUTOR

Lora Jarocki lives in Oklahoma with her fiancé and their bulldog, Brutus. Her job has a non-disclosure agreement and in her off time she is trying to perfect the chocolate chip cookie.

*"Attitude is a little thing
that makes a big difference."*

Winston Churchill

– 31 –

Burnt Biscuits

contributed by Art Ernst

NOTE: We found this story floating around the Internet in different forms, "author unknown." A bit of detective work by our own Chris Neck turned up the original author, original story, and some very cool background.

Heat up some coffee. Savor this moment. You're in for a treat.

We'll start with the email Chris received from the now 85-year-old author. Then, in its original form, enjoy one of the most touching dad stories (and best life lessons) you'll ever read.

Chris,

I am 85 and my mother died in 1966. I wrote this article a number of years ago. I had entered it in a contest (which I didn't win), but all entries were published.

My article about the burned biscuits took on a life of its own. I had originally called it "A Lesson Learned at Breakfast 80 Years Ago." Since then, I have been receiving it from various places. Some have changed it from breakfast to supper. Others have left out portions or added to it.

I will send you my complete article as written years ago. The article in its travels has usually been signed "author unknown" or "anonymous." But since it is a tribute to my Dad, I'm more than happy to see it floating around.

I originally wrote it to and for my three children, to pass on to their children. Since my printer is on the blink, I'll just add it to this letter.

You may ... use it in its entirety, partially, or not at all.

Cordially,

Art Ernst

A Lesson at Breakfast 80 Years Ago

When I was a little boy five years of age, living on the farm, Mama liked to start the day right by cooking a tasteful breakfast, usually at 5:00 a.m.

One morning, so long ago, Mama placed a plate of fried eggs and bacon and fried apples in front of all the family, and placed an extremely burned plate of biscuits in the center of the table.

I remember waiting to see if Dad would notice. But all he did was reach for a biscuit, as he smiled at Mama.

I remember watching him smear butter and jelly on that ugly burned biscuit. He ate every bite of that thing ... never made a face or said a word about it.

When I got up from the table that morning, I remember hearing Mama apologize to Dad for burning the biscuits. And I'll never forget what he said: "Honey, I love burned biscuits every now and then."

Later that morning, I asked him if he really liked his biscuits burned.

He wrapped me in his arms and said, "Your Mama puts in a hard day at work every day, and she gets tired. There's just as much love in a burned biscuit as there is in an unburned one. And besides, a little burned biscuit every now and then never hurt anybody!"

As I've grown older, I've thought about that morning many times. Life is not always fair, and it is full of imperfect things and imperfect people, and I'm not perfect.

I forget things like everybody else. But what I've learned over the years, is that learning to accept each other's faults and choosing to celebrate each other's differences is one of the most important keys to creating healthy, growing, and lasting relationships.

Throughout our married life, if my wife, Jane, burned something, I'd say, 'Sweetheart, I like it that way."

A loving family—seated: Jane and Art; their children, standing, from left: Rick, Heather, and Randy

Which I really did, as she prepared it out of love. All her food has one main ingredient: LOVE.

And that's my wish for each of my children and grand-children: that you will learn to take the good, bad, and ugly parts of your life and overcome them with kindness. Because in the end, true thoughtfulness, forgiveness, and consideration will give you a relationship where a burnt biscuit ain't such a big deal!

This can be extended to any relationship. In fact, under-standing is the real basis of all relationships, be it brother-sister, husband-wife, parent-child, partners, or just plain old friendship! Learn to be resilient.

Be kinder than necessary because everybody you meet is fighting some kind of battle.

Don't put the key to your happiness in someone else's pocket—keep it in your own.

So, "please pass me a biscuit," and yeah, the burned one will be just fine! Remember: "As rain and sunshine

Art and Jane at a church function

nourish the flowers, so praise and encouragement nourishes the human spirit." This is the lesson I learned at breakfast 80 years ago.

Thanks, Dad!

With everlasting love, to Rick, Randy, and Heather, and all the Grands.

ABOUT THE CONTRIBUTOR

Art Ernst lives in a retirement home in Nebraska with his wife of 57 years, Jane. Art is a former Methodist minister who now enjoys writing poetry and visiting with his three children and seven grandchildren.

"It's not easy being a mother.
If it were easy, fathers would do it."

The Golden Girls

– 32 –

My Dad's Name Was Mom

contributed by Brandon Steiner

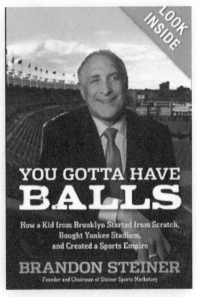

You Gotta Have Balls is Brandon Steiner's inspiring book about growing as a dirt-poor Jewish boy, with no dad and no money. He and his mom got by on welfare stamps.

Things worked out. Today, his Steiner Sports is a multi-million dollar international brand, the heaviest hitter in the sports memorabilia world. Brandon is also a big-hearted guy and a valued, "What can I do for you?" personal friend. How did he do it? "My mom," Brandon proudly tells Savvy Dad.

"I had no dad. We had no money. But Mom took no excuses. She was forced to wear the 'dad hat,' and she wore it well. Mom would say, "I'm your mom and your dad too, so whatever I say goes double!"

Brandon's mom,
Evelyn Steiner

We asked Brandon to share the most valuable lessons he learned from this remarkable woman who served as both mom and dad. He asked that we share three, and you don't mess with kids from Brooklyn, so here they are:

Lesson #1—Be an Advocate, Not a Judge

Mom was incredibly giving, despite our lack of money. It seemed like the less we had, the more she would try to give away! One day, as we were walking home from the market, she placed a whole dollar into the cup of a homeless guy. I quietly snuck back to pull the dollar from his cup, but Mom caught me in the act. After demanding that I immediately put the dollar back in the cup, she pulled me aside and said, "Brandon, it's not for you to judge who needs help and who doesn't.

"If a person asks for help, you help them, plain and simple. Unless you sit on a bench in a black robe, your job is not to judge others, especially those in need."

Mom's lesson took. I try to help people whenever I can. I don't question their need. I don't ask why. I'm an advocate of help, not a judge of needs.

Lesson #2—It's Not What Happens; It's How You React

Fourth grade. Mr. Kerper's class. He also lived across the street from us. An athlete in his heyday. A tall, well built man. All the kids looked up to him. I sure did. Mr. Kerper asked me to remain after class one day. He asked, "Brandon, you've been wearing the same pants for the past three weeks now. Do you have another pair, son?"

It was true. I was so embarrassed. I tried to lie my way out of it. "No Mr. Kerper, I wore different ones last week," I defended. "Well, does that other pair of pants have the same rip in the right knee?" he questioned, pointing to the tear in the leg of my pants.

Busted cold! I froze, speechless.

"Here," he continued, pulling a few bills from his wallet. "Take this home to your mom for some new pants."

Money in hand, I ran home, crying the whole way. I was mortified. "Why are you so upset?" Mom asked when I got home. I explained what happened. "Now Mr. Kerper knows we're poor!" I moaned.

"Brandon, it's not about what happens to you, it's about how you react. I'm sorry about what happened today, but there is no reason to be upset. Take this money back to Mr. Kerper tomorrow and tell him, 'Thank you, but there are others who need the money more than we do.' We'll get you new pants next week when the welfare check arrives."

This was a valuable lesson from Mom.

Embarrassing, seemingly unexpected, things are going to happen. Expect it. You can't control that. But you can control how you react.

Lesson #3 — Be Accountable; Earn the Right to Accept Help

The Kerper incident was a turning point for me. Still bothered, I asked Mom about it later that day.

"Accepting help from others is OK if you really need it," she said, "but you must be accountable. You've got to earn the right to accept help. If you don't do what you can to avoid needing help, you don't deserve the help."

The following Saturday, I hit the streets in search of a job. I was 10. Eight long hours on the hunt … nothing. As a fourth grader, I didn't have much of a resume yet. The end of the day. One last shot — Freddie the Fruit Man. I had asked him for a delivery job earlier that day. He laughed at me.

I went back for another attempt, begging Freddie with all that I had. To my surprise, he actually said yes! I sprinted home, "Mom! I got it! I got a job! You don't need to worry about me anymore!"

She smiled, amused. "OK, just after school and on weekends though," she warned. "You are accountable. I am proud of you."

Three lessons from Mom:

Don't judge those in need.

It's not what happens; it's how we react.

Be accountable before you accept help.

My mom raised three proud, successful men on her own. On welfare. Living principles like these. My mom — the best dad a kid could have.

About the Contributor

Brandon Steiner is an author, motivational speaker, and CEO of Steiner Sports Marketing, based in New Rochelle, N.Y. He has written two books, including his most recent, *You Gotta Have Balls: How a Kid from Brooklyn Started From Scratch, Bought Yankee Stadium, and Created a Sports Empire.*

You can read Brandon's daily insights into business, relationships and life on his blog at *BrandonSteiner.com*

> *"The only true wisdom
> is in knowing you know nothing."*
>
> Socrates

– 33 –

Chubby Rules

by Greg Hague

I've been fortunate. Most of my life, I've been surrounded by people with smarts.

It started with my dad, Chubby. He taught me a ton and made me want to know more.

I learned that big concepts can often be expressed in just a few words. Chubby was a master at that.

Over 30+ years, I've assembled quite a collection of these nuggets of life. I call them "Chubby Rules," named after my dad.

Greg, 1966, a high school senior

Following are a few of my favorites.

You can accomplish anything if you don't care who gets the credit.

When I was younger I was close to obsessed with wanting others to recognize my efforts, to give me credit for what I had done. When they would say, "Good job" with a pat on the back, I worked double hard to prove they were right. Later in life I began thinking more about credit to others than credit to me. What a difference that made!

When you tell others you trust them, they usually bust their butt to prove you are right.

The key is not to just trust others; it's letting them know.

It's stressful when a client, partner, or friend says, "Greg, you make the decision. I trust you will do what's fair." What a burden!

Of course, I would have been fair. Now I have to be more than fair to prove I'm not shading it my way. I'm often unfair to me to ensure I'm being fair to them.

Tex, a dear friend, once wrote this reference for me, "I would trust Greg with my wife and my checkbook." He treats everyone that way, with complete trust, unless they prove they're not deserving. It's a big reason why he's built one of the largest automobile dealership networks in the nation.

I am not that good; I am that prepared.

I've learned that in business, law, parenting, and life, having a natural "gift" is nice. But knowing your stuff ten times better than the other guy smokes talent most every time.

When you look forward to lunch, you need a new job.

My last few years in the real estate business taught me that. I had done it too long. I was burned out. The highlight each day was "where are we going for lunch." I did it well, but it was no longer challenging, no longer fun. It was simply a way to make money.

Fast forward to today. I've learned that when you are excited about what you do all day, lunch is just something that gets in the way.

Most people look for a great job. Too few look for a great idea.

I've done a fair amount of public speaking, often to college students. I'm always surprised at how many are 100% focused on simply getting a job.

Very few ask me to talk about how they can form a shoe-string entrepreneurial venture and build something of their own, something they can be proud of. It seems to me that if there was ever a time in a person's life when they could afford to take a risk, right out of school would be it.

Most aren't married. Few have kids. "So what" if they fall on their face? At that age they have much to gain and little to lose.

The solution to worrying is to start doing.

Worrying is a worthless exercise. With any problem, the worst thing you can do is nothing. Better to choose wrong than choose nothing. At least if you choose wrong, you're likely to figure out what's right.

A problem is a set of facts compounded by emotion.

Clients often don't need my law knowledge, they need my objectivity. From outside their emotional "forest," I look at the facts, set out their various courses of action, and then let them choose. They may not like the options, but the best one is usually obvious. They didn't see it because they were caught up in the emotions of anger, hurt, disappointment or fear.

Want to solve a problem? Get rid of the emotion. Lay out the facts. Make a decision. Don't look back.

Chubby Hague

A TRIBUTE TO CHUBBY

If you'd like a list of "Chubby Rules," send me an email. I love to share—

Greg@SavvyDad.com

*"If you don't think every day is a good day,
just try missing one."*
Cavett Robert

– 34 –

Squaring Off
the Curve

contributed by Dr. Kenneth Cooper

My father, a practicing dentist for some 50 years, was intensely interested in the prevention of disease as compared to just treatment.

When I was applying for medical school, my dad told me that if all I would be doing in the future was taking care of people by ordering drugs, he was wasting his time and money. That is one reason I redirected my medical practice from "too much care too late" to *prevention* of disease.

Dad said, "It is always cheaper and more efficient to maintain good health than regain it once it is lost."

My father practiced his specialty of dentistry all day on a Friday and died on a Monday. We call that "squaring off the curve." It's living a long, healthy life to the fullest, and then dying suddenly.

Certainly, my mother "squared off the curve." Back in 1984, she voted in the presidential election. She returned

Retired quarterback Troy Aikman, Mrs. Angie and Dr. Kenneth Cooper, and theologian Dr. Russell Dilday at an event reception

to her home in Oklahoma City and the next morning we found her stretched out on the sofa. The television was still on. She was wearing a lapel pin that said "I voted today."

At 83 years of age, she was living in her own home, fully independent, driving her own car. What she feared more than death was losing her independence.

The stories about my dad and my mom "squaring off the curve" are what motivated me and my son, Tyler, to collaborate on the book, *Start Strong, Finish Strong*. Many have told us it inspired them to change their lives.

Because what could be a greater success than to square off your own curve?

ABOUT THE CONTRIBUTOR

Dr. Cooper is known world-wide for inventing the term "aerobics." He authored the 1968 book by the same name and launched a health movement that swept the land and endures to this day.

According to Cooper, "The goal of medicine should be to keep you healthy, not to provide too much care too late."

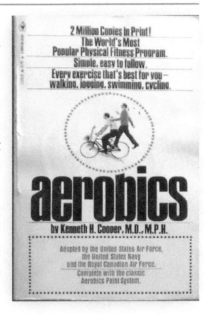

*"Dear Past, thank you for your lessons.
Dear Future, I'm ready.
Dear God, thank you for giving me
another chance."*

Author Unknown

– 35 –

Mom's Second Life

contributed by Yonsenia White

She almost died. That's why she lived.

My mother, Mrs. Arnetta White. Born in poverty. The youngest of twelve. She faced racism, sexism, segregation, and a troubled marriage, as well.

After Dad left, Mom filled both parenting roles. She shined at both. We rarely felt an absence of Dad. She never complained. Her strength of character and faith in God got us all through some difficult times. Her heart was so big, her effort so great. She made many sacrifices for us. And in all of my life, I've seen Mom cry only twice.

She raised my brothers and me on a housekeeper's salary. Her venue each day? Twenty-some rooms on a nursing home floor. Climbing ladders. Changing curtains. Mopping floors. Removing trash. For anyone, especially a heavyset woman of 60, backbreaking work.

Then it happened. Mom suddenly became tired, light-headed, but wanted to finish her housekeeping duties.

The White family in 1974: Keith (seated), Kevin (standing),
Arnetta (mother), Henry (father), and Yonsenia as a baby

When she got home, she felt a lot worse. My brother rushed her to the hospital.

"If you hadn't come to the hospital when you did," the doctor said, "you'd be dead."

Mom had been having a heart attack all day. We didn't know then. We do now. Mom was diagnosed with congestive heart failure and told to lose the weight that had taxed her heart for many years. She was faced with a choice. Create a new life—or have none at all.

Drug therapy, weight loss, exercise, a strict low sodium diet. She struggled to lose weight and was advised to undergo gastrointestinal surgery for immediate results. She lost over 200 pounds, going from size 34 to a 14.

Before and after: Arnetta White's pre-surgery self in January 2000, and 6 years after surgery, in December 2010, looking fit and trim

With a renewed body and healing heart, Mom's now the picture of health. My mom of the past expired that day. A new one emerged, with twice the spunk and *joie de vivre* as before. And now, at 70, Mom has retired from house-keeping, as an award-winning employee of 30 years. With five grandchildren, Mom has five more reasons to live.

What did I learn from my mom (who as a single mom was also my dad)?

Life presents us with many struggles. When we fall down, we have to get up.

And when it comes to our health, we must have the discipline to take care of the bodies we've been given, no matter what stage of life.

For Mom, it took a second chance at life to appreciate and act on that message. But for many, there is no second bite at the apple. They never get that "do-over," like my mom did.

ABOUT THE CONTRIBUTOR

Yonsenia White is a graduate of Homer L. Ferguson High School in Newport News, Virginia, and an alumnus of Virginia Tech and Rutgers University. She is currently working on her Masters of Science in Art Therapy and Counseling at Eastern Virginia Medical School in Norfolk, Virginia. She is a tenured professor of studio art and a professional artist. Her website is www.yonseniawhite.com.

Arnetta's 2012 retirement party

Yonsenia's mom, Arnetta White, is a native of Newport News, Virginia, and a graduate of George W. Carver High School. She has four children and five grandchildren. Mrs. White is now retired after 30 years working as a housekeeper in the Riverside Regional Health System.

"The weak can never forgive. Forgiveness is the attribute of the strong."

Mahatma Gandhi

– 36 –

The Thief

contributed by Sam Rasoul

Dad's nightmare had just walked through the door, a masked man there to rob his store.

As a convenience store owner, few figures were more terrifying. It was a rough neighborhood. Some had been shot.

Dad saw no weapon, but the man's menacing tone was scary enough. He instructed Dad to hand over the cash. Dad's hands trembled as he pulled the bills from the drawer.

As the clandestine thief turned to rush out, something flashed in

Sam's dad, Ralph Rasoul

Dad's mind. Was it the gait? The voice? He realized he knew who it was!

"Abraham," he called out, but it was too late. This man he knew was gone, as were Dad's earnings that day.

Owning a small business was a triumph for Dad. He had emigrated from Palestine years before. Strange culture. New language. Long, grueling hours in the store. With a wife and four kids, he had barely scraped by. This was a devastating loss.

Everyone in the local housing projects counted on him. They relied on his credit to feed their families between paychecks. This day would hurt not only Dad, but his ability to help them, as well.

My father should have been enraged at the thief. This was a man he had helped. But Dad only felt sad. He felt pity for a man who was so desperate, a man who had to resort to something so low.

When the police came, Dad protested. He didn't want them to arrest Abraham. He pitied this man, but the police insisted. Justice had to be done. Abraham was found, handcuffed and taken away.

On the morning of Abraham's trial, he stopped by Dad's store. He told my dad how awful he felt, how hungry he had been, and asked for forgiveness.

Dad gave him a hug, then gave him something to eat. With not a penny for bus fair, my dad also gave him a ride to the court.

At the hearing, Dad spoke eloquently on Abraham's behalf. Although he would do a bit of jail time, when Abraham was released, Dad helped him once again.

What did I learn from my dad?

He was tough. He made it despite the odds. What most paved his way? Dad has a remarkable heart.

Like his dreams, his kindness to others could not be crushed. He believed then, as he does to this day, that those who hurt you still deserve love and another chance.

That is Dad's way.

ABOUT THE CONTRIBUTOR

Sam Rasoul is the youngest person in history to run for U.S. Congress. He and his wife knocked on 30,000 doors in 22 months. Sam ultimately lost, but scored more votes than any other against his 17-year congressional incumbent.

Sam obtained his MBA and is now the Chief Operating Officer of a major international charity. Putting the lessons he learned from his dad into practice, Sam devotes his days to traveling the globe, meeting world leaders, and helping others in life.

"As human beings, we have the ability, and the choice, to lift people up or to put them down."

Bob Burg

– 37 –

Meet the Master of Goodspeak

contributed by Bob Burg

Wise words from Bob Burg—and he would know. He's made a career of uplifting others, while teaching them, in turn, to do the same.

Bob shares his wisdom in best-selling books like *Endless Referrals* and *The Go-Giver*. He inspires jam-packed audiences including Fortune 500 companies.

Bob's dad, Mike, taught him a key lesson on life … Goodspeak.

Mike is the Master of "Goodspeak."

Goodspeak?

Goodspeak, a word Bob made up, means finding the best in people—and vocalizing it. "Most people gossip. Dad finds and speaks the good," says Bob.

But it's more than just kindness and compliments. Goodspeak is about setting an example. To Bob, that's essential to the "lifting up"—as you're about to see.

Here's what Bob says about his dad, The Master of Goodspeak:

Have you ever heard husbands, when speaking to others, make unkind remarks about their wives? It's one of those macho things, right?

Sure, they're "only kidding," but words matter. Examples, good and bad, are set, especially for children.

Mike, my dad, ALWAYS speaks of Mom in the most complimentary, glowing terms. As does she of him. They began poor and built a successful business.

Although Dad was the one in the public eye and Mom more comfortable behind the scenes, Dad always made sure everyone knew that Mom was the driving force.

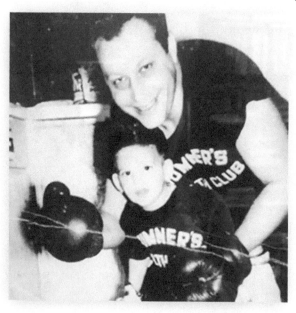

Bob's dad, Mike, giving Bob his first boxing lesson; after World War II ended, Mike ran the famous 5th Street Gym in Miami Beach, Florida

My favorite "Dad story" took place when I was 12. We were having carpet installed in our home.

The crew boss was one of those stereotypical beer-guzzlin', hard-livin' guys, who would have probably belonged to Ralph Kramden's Raccoon Lodge from the old Honeymooner's TV show (nothing wrong with that—just painting a picture).

For lunch, my folks bought pizza for the crew. Dad went to talk with the boss about the job. I was listening in, just around the corner.

The boss said, 'This is an expensive job. Women will really spend your money, won't they?"

Dad responded, "Well, I'll tell you, when they were right there with you before you had money, it's a pleasure to do anything you can for them now."

This wasn't the answer the crew boss expected. He was looking for negative talk about wives, which to him was normal.

He tried again, "But, gee, they'll really play off that and spend all they can, won't they?"

Dad replied, as I knew he would, "Hey, when they're the reason you're successful, you want them to have and do what they enjoy."

Please understand; Dad did not speak in a condescending manner. He was simply being himself; a man who loved and respected his wife (my Mom) so much that there was no way he would give in and participate in that type of talk.

Finally, the boss gave up. Maybe he learned something about respecting one's spouse. Maybe not. But it taught a young boy a lot about the power of respect.

Goodspeak.

Saying positive words. Uplifting others. Inspiring them to do the same. That's my dad. I strive to follow his example!

About the Contributor

Bob Burg is a highly sought-after speaker at corporate, sales, and entrepreneurial conventions. He speaks on the principles contained in his two most well-known books, *Endless Referrals* and *The Go-Giver*. Four of Bob's books have sold over 250,000 copies each. His website is *burg.com*.

Mike, the Master of Goodspeak, with his son, Bob

"To a father growing old, nothing is dearer than a daughter."

-Euripides

— 38 —

Jilted in Prague

contributed by Courtney Cee

People can be jerks. Let's call this jerk "Brad."

He was not my first love, but he was my first jerk.

I was 23. Brad did a number on me.

I was teaching English in Prague, living far from my home in the U.S. I had just been jilted by a jerk named Brad.

It felt like I'd been kicked to the curb. Sitting at the top of a staircase, I had been spying on Brad. What I observed, I hated, but expected. It was not what I hoped.

My dad had just flown in for a visit. He didn't know. The moment I saw him, I crumbled.

"Brad stole my heart, Dad. He siphoned my money, took all that I had. We dated a few months. He said he was temporarily short. I started picking up tabs. He said he lost his job. I opened my home.

"While I worked, he emptied my pantry and kept the couch warm. Then left me.

"Once I was tapped out, he found a new softy to use."

My dad was a bank inspector. Reserved. The resolute, silent type. You need to know that to appreciate what occurred next. Dad's look was like never before. Could eyes glisten with warmth while raging in fury? With as loving a voice as I'd ever heard, he soothed, "I'm so sorry, honey. Heartbreak can be part of life."

"I need to see him one more time," I told Dad, sniffling. Brad had my prized books. We arranged to meet at a café nearby.

"Tell him to come here, sweetheart," Dad said. "I'll take care of it for you."

I agreed. Arrangements were made. Soon after, a call from the lobby told us Brad had arrived.

Courtney and her dad, John, in Rich Valley, Virginia

"I'll be right back," Dad firmly said. The door shut as he left.

I couldn't stay away. I was consumed with curiosity. Would Brad be upset that I had not personally come? Would he bring all my things? What would Dad say?

Head low, I snuck down the hallway to the top of the stairs. A muffled exchange of voices came from below. I gulped. I crouched. I peered through the bannister, unseen from above. I looked down on Dad's back. Brad faced him, arms filled with books.

The earth suddenly shook. My quiet father was quiet no more.

"What the hell were you doing?" Dad bellowed.

This normally reserved father
stood up for his daughter

It was a thunderous roar. This was Dad like never before! "You led her on. You used her. You don't treat a woman like that. You will never say a word to my little girl again."

My eyes bulged and grew wide.

"You're going to get exactly what's coming to you. I'm just the guy to make that happen. You don't deserve to be on the same planet with my girl. You are an inconsiderate mooch."

Brad sputtered some lame excuse. What a mistake! Dad blew him away.

"I don't want to hear it. Grow up. Grow a pair. Give me those books. Get out of my way."

I scurried back to the room as fast as I could. I was crying a bit. I was smiling a heck of a lot more.

Dad returned in moments, books in his arms. He laid them down gently. I rinsed my face. We had a quiet dinner.

Never did he say a word. Nor did I—until now.

ABOUT THE CONTRIBUTOR

Courtney Cee is a librarian in Southwest Virginia. She is a fan of literature, animals, art, and of course, her dad.

*"You can have everything you want in life
if you just help enough people get
what they want in life."*

Zig Ziglar

– 39 –

Chit Capital

by Greg Hague

Millions of words exist on how to make it in life.

Chubby taught it in few. Here are two: chit capital.

In 1962, I wanted to start my first business. I was 14 and needed 75 bucks to buy a lawn mower.

The marketing strategy? Door to door with a flyer.

"I Cut Grass. Good. Cheap. Greg."

When I asked Dad to loan me the $75, he asked why. I knew my dad. I was prepared and told him my plan.

Chubby thought for a minute. He pulled out his money clip and counted out 75 bucks. He spread it on the table and walked away.

Are you kidding? I thought. What was going on? No piercing questions? No third degree. This was not what I expected.

Dad had always stressed a thing called "quid pro quo", doing a "this" in exchange for a "that." I do something for you if you do something for me. I loan you money if you pay me interest.

My weekly allowance was the quid pro quo for doing my chores. Want a quarter for the ice cream truck? The quid pro quo was sweeping the driveway.

But this $75? What did he want in return?

Perplexed, I went running after Dad.

"Hey Dad," I said, "What's the quid pro quo for the 75 bucks?"

"It's chit capital," he said, as he continued to walk. At that moment I should have known. My father was at it again, trying to find an unusual way to mentor me with one of his "rules of life." I took the bait.

"What's chit capital?" I asked.

"Greg, a chit is when you do nice, but don't ask for nice back. When you do lots of nice, you build chit capital."

The Hague home in Cincinnati, where Greg first learned about "chit capital"

Right off the bat, I could see the problem with that. "Dad," I said, thinking quickly, "With this $75, how will I know when I've paid enough nice back?" Chubby responded with a victorious smile, "You won't." He turned and walked away.

I remember thinking, this is one of the worst deals I've ever made. An undefined burden. Chubby had outsmarted me for years. He'd just done it again.

Okay, chalk it to inexperience. I was only 14. But my father taught me to learn from my mistakes. So, I bought a little red book. I called it my Chit Diary.

I started doing nice for everyone and writing it down. Just like Dad. I was going to build up lots of chit capital. My sister, Linda, told me "forget it," she'd "never do nice back."

That got me thinking. Would people remember? Would I ever get paid back? I didn't see anyone making notes in an "I owe Greg" diary.

Greg's sister, Linda, was an Olympic-level equestrian, but she wasn't buying the concept of "chit capital"

So, I asked Chubby about that. Here's what he said:

"Greg, you're thinking about it the wrong way. When you get paid back, you lose. That chit comes off your list. You go backwards."

Dad was so smart. Do lots of nice. Ask nothing back. Live rich in chit capital. Die the same way.

Chit capital. It's a smart move and makes legacies, too.

"The only place success comes before work is in the dictionary."

Vince Lombardi

– 40 –

Best $2 I Never Earned

contributed by David Vogt

Friday was payday!

I had just turned six. I was building a barn in rural Illinois, working for Dad. He was paying me 50¢ an hour.

David working for his dad at 50¢ per hour

Dad's "day job" was as a factory worker. He made screws for telephones. Back then, he needed to moonlight construction to support our family. Eventually he rose into management, a high-paying job. But this was long before then.

That week, he was pouring a concrete floor for a barn. It was backbreaking labor.

I was Dad's little helper, a "gofer," he said. For a six-year-old, the worksite was full of temptation, like furrowing dirt "roads" for the toy trucks I brought along.

As Dad worked on the barn, my imaginary "crew" zoomed over my miniature roads. I had a ball. Dad was so nice. He said not a word.

As we wrapped up on Friday, I tallied my pay at eight bucks. Sixteen hours of "kind-of" hard work. I watched as Dad slapped down my bills.

Oops, only $6, I thought. He owed me two more.

Official uniform of Dad's Building Company

"Dad," I said, (feeling rather proud to show off my advanced math), "I worked 16 hours this week. That's eight bucks, not six."

The boss didn't blink.

"David," he said, "You spent four hours on roads, twelve on the barn. You don't get paid for work you don't do."

I pouted a lot, but knew he was right. It made quite an impression, even at that very young age. Reflecting back, it was the best two bucks I never earned.

Today, I'm an HR Business Partner in the People Department for Southwest Airlines. My charge: the development of strong leaders, teams, and organizations. I have a family of my own, and I still look to my dad as my model in life.

I've long since put away my toy trucks, but I'll never forget the lesson I learned. The two bucks I never earned taught me that quality of work determines quantity of return.

David and his dad in front of the car he later bought with money he earned

David and Bill Vogt

ABOUT THE CONTRIBUTOR

Dave Vogt is an HR Business Partner with Southwest Airlines. A native of Illinois, he attended Illinois State University, where he obtained a BS in Criminal Justice. Dave is the father of three, and the husband of one. He and his wife celebrated 20 years of marriage last year.

"Sometimes you will never know the true value of a moment until it becomes a memory."

Author Unknown

– 41 –

One More Day

contributed by Mike Stewart

One more day. With your father. Your son. What would you give? I sat on the edge of Mark's hospice bed, his hand in mine. I gently brushed the thin, wispy hair back from his forehead. "He's gone," the nurse whispered from behind. The words I had feared for five years.

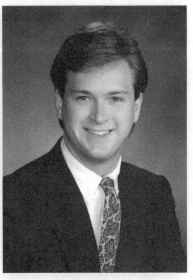

Mike's wonderful son, Mark, before his illness

I have never understood why my son's fate was to die young. I don't expect that I will. My name is Mike Stewart. This is the story of Mark. He was my son.

So bright, so funny. A regular comedian, and smart as a whip. Successful, respected in his professional career. Mark was that one person in anyone's life, that one person who makes you believe, who gives you hope, who pulls you through.

But cancer doesn't discriminate. The diagnosis was real. A parent's worst fear. "Not Mark. Please, God, anything but this. Don't take my son." But I had to be strong. Together, we had to beat this thing. But I was terrified, as any father would be.

Where did I find my strength? In Mark. Never once did he ask, "Why me?"

"Dad, we're all living on borrowed time. Most people live dying. They die a little bit every day. I'm going to die

living. Every day I will learn something new, do things for others, and make the world laugh."

It's been 15 years. It feels like months. But Mark's example lives on through those who he touched in the time that he had.

There is an old saying (popularized by the movie *The Last Samurai*):

"Tell me how he died."

"I will tell you how he lived."

And live he did. Mark is my "Last Samurai." Others feel the same.

The pain of loss is still sharp today, but I don't dwell on it. Mark wouldn't stand for that. Mark taught me many lessons in those last five years. Above all, he taught me the delicacy of life.

Appreciate who you have. Your kids. Your mom and dad. Your friends. Your wife. The time together. Each hour. Each day.

We take it for granted, don't we?

I love you, son.

About the Contributor

Mike Stewart, CSP, RCC, is President of Stewart & Stewart, Inc. (DBA Mike Stewart Sales Dynamics), an Atlanta-based firm focused on hiring and developing high performance sales teams. Mike speaks and writes on contemporary sales, sales management, and personal achievement issues.

*"I'm not afraid of storms, for I'm learning
to sail my ship."*

Aeschylus

– 42 –

Prove Dad Wrong

contributed by Tom Hopkins

As a student, I was never at the top of my class. Still, my parents struggled to save money to send me to college. I dutifully attended — for 90 days — then decided it wasn't for me. I quit and went home.

After their sacrifice, my parents weren't pleased with my decision. My father told me, "Son, I will always love you. But, you will never amount to anything without a college education."

My father was a strong man. I had never seen him cry. Tears filled his eyes as he said those words.

But Dad didn't realize the gift he gave me that day. He ignited a burning desire to prove he was wrong. I determined that, whatever it took, I would succeed without a college education.

I had to work a backbreaking labor job to pay bills, but I was on a quest. I was determined to find my gift, my purpose in life.

And my father during those difficult times? The dad who said I'd never succeed helped me virtually every day.

Les Hopkins and his successful young son, Tom

Finally, I found my niche selling real estate. My parents saw how hard I worked. They gave me the money to buy a car. It wasn't a great car, but it was better than trying to sell real estate from the back of my motorcycle. I worked night and day and enjoyed tremendous success. That led to the worldwide training career I enjoy today. Dad's kick in the butt and help on the way made it all happen.

Over the years, I've discovered a truth. Most successful people were motivated to prove something to someone, at some time in their life (even if just to themselves).

Perhaps they were told they "weren't worthy" of success. Or maybe, without college they'd never succeed. It doesn't matter what they were told.

What matters is this. That was the moment they flipped the switch.

Nothing and no one would stand in their way. My dad knew just what to say.

I bought my parents a retirement home on a golf course as a token of my tremendous thanks. It was my dad's life-long dream to play golf whenever he wanted. That's how he spent his last days on earth. Dad enjoyed the rewards of that drive for success he ignited in me.

About the Contributor

Since 1976, Tom Hopkins has dedicated his professional life to providing cutting edge sales training strategies and techniques to individuals and corporations around the world. He is a coveted motivational speaker and bestselling author.

"Tell me and I forget.
Teach me and I remember.
Involve me and I learn."

-Benjamin Franklin

— 43 —

Chubby Right

by Greg Hague

It's painful to recall that icy-cold night when Mimi so hopelessly cried. And my father acted so badly.

It was the winter of '63. I was 15. Chubby asked if I'd like to sit in on one of his new agent real estate training sessions. He held them three nights a week in the conference room at the office.

What "boss's son" wouldn't? This would be totally fun. Soon, I would learn it would be the opposite of fun.

Every new agent attended. A doctor's note was your only excuse.

Chubby started the evening by calling on a sweet, middle aged, soft-spoken lady named Mimi. He asked her to stand. "Mimi," he said, "Give us the definition of real estate." She did. It was totally right, just not word-for-word perfect—what I came to call "Chubby Right."

"Mimi, do it again, and do it just right," Dad ordered, with a suddenly harsh tone. She did. It was perfectly right, just not word-for-word perfect, not Chubby Right.

It was like the movie *Groundhog Day*. Over and over she tried, over and over he replied, "You will do it just right, or we'll be here all night."

I was aghast. I looked around the room. The trainees were petrified—about to pee in their pants. Who would be next? Might I? You've heard the phrase "the fear was palpable." This was much worse.

"Perfect and right," a motto of Chubby's

It went on and on, and on. Mimi's soft face was shiny, beet-red with floods of big tears streaking her cheeks. Her eyes were aglow with fear.

I was horrified. I was embarrassed. Chubby wouldn't let up.

Then, abruptly it came to an end. Dad's face turned suddenly warm. His piercing blue eyes deepened in tone. He pulled out his hankie, strode out into the room, and walked over to Mimi.

He gave her a hug, wiped her moist cheeks, and respectfully said, "Mimi, I won't say I'm sorry, because I'm honestly not. This business is frequently brutal and terribly tough. You are the kind of good-hearted, caring person we so desperately need. But, to show us the way, you've got to be brilliant. You've got to know everything perfectly right. Let's try it again tomorrow night."

With that, Chubby turned to the class and casually said, "Tomorrow everyone, perfect and right."

Out in the car I said not a word—no clue what to say. After a moment, Dad spoke with a serious tone, "Greg, some day people will count on you for advice. You need to know how to guide them right. Most people give lousy advice because they know what they know mushy and weak. Please, son, don't march to their beat."

It was so true. Most of what I knew, I knew "kind of, sort of." It was the same with most of my friends. I determined that this would no longer be me.

I decided that I would darn well know what I knew with absolute clarity, perfectly right. No mush. "No oatmeal," as I often say to my law students and others I teach.

What about Mimi? She made millions and rose to the top. She strove to know everything perfect and right—what we together affectionately called Chubby Right. And, she stood by Dad's side until the day he died.

A lesson on learning. A lesson on life. No oatmeal. Most people learn narrow and wide. Know what you know narrow and deep, what Mimi and I call Chubby Right.

One of Chubby's billboards—his firm really did deliver
"matchless performance"

Chubby would be proud of his "Chubby Right" grandsons—
Corey, Brian, Casey, and Jason

*"Optimism is the faith that leads to achievement.
Nothing can be done
without hope and confidence."*

Helen Keller

– 44 –

Long Walk
Without Shoes

contributed by Shawn Kumar

A long walk without shoes. A craggy dirt road.

An hour to school. An hour back home.

My name is Shawn Kumar. This is about Dad.

What kids now expect, he would never have dreamed. My father grew up in India. He was thankful just to have shoes. As hard as it was, Dad dreamed of the best, only good things. He did it back then. He does it today.

My father was determined to create an opportunity-filled life for the family he one day would have.

He committed himself to do what it took. He knew it would be hard. Dad studied and worked night into day. At 21, he earned a scholarship to travel from India to attend college in the U.S. By just 34, he had saved enough to start his own business.

He worked with intensity, vision, courage and heart. But life can be good, then turn suddenly bad.

It was June 1991. I was just seven. Dad's business was flourishing. He had worked hard with a positive attitude and warm, caring heart. His firm would eventually grow to almost 2000 employees—$230 million annually in revenue.

At the time, I was a Chicago Bulls fanatic, just like my dad. Celebrating our team's first NBA Championship, we were shooting hoops in the driveway. He suddenly vanished into the house. A water break, I thought?

Minutes passed. He didn't return. I wanted to play, so I ran in to bring him back outside.

A son's worst nightmare lay on the floor. Dad stretched out, writhing in pain. I was scared beyond anything I can describe in mere words. I quickly called 911. Dad had

Nand and Shawn Kumar ...

suffered "the widow maker," so dubbed because it is often fatal. Only 2% of victims survive. Those who do may live only a year.

In the hospital, he looked up silently, his eyes full of tears. My father saw our fearful faces. He could barely speak, but later he told me, "Shawn, I could pray."

"One more year," he asked, "Let me have one more year to teach my children all that I've learned. They are too young. I will not leave them this way."

Dad later told me that he visualized his arteries rebuilding. He imagined purified blood rushing through his heart. He could picture the damaged tissue healing. He made up his mind to live, to be strong again.

The first few weeks were scary and tough. We didn't know if Dad would make it. He could barely shower or

... proud dad with proud son

walk. But his belief in recovery never wavered; his mind drove the healing inside.

My dad is the most positive, committed man in the world. Time and time again, he does what it takes to make dreams come true.

Those long shoeless walks to never miss school. The scholarship he earned to come to the U.S. The business he built. The way he healed his heart.

I am a fortunate son. I now work with my dad. Each day is a gift. He has taught me so much.

I'm not the only one who appreciates the gift of this man. While many businesses laid people off during the post-2008 downturn, Dad never let go of a single employee. He just wouldn't do it. He'd work late into the night, and didn't quit until he found a way.

My father approaches every issue with a smile on his face, a pat on the back, believing in nothing but success and brighter times.

The right outlook. The grit to do what it takes. That is my dad. That is the great lesson I will pass on to my son one day.

ABOUT THE CONTRIBUTOR

Shawn Kumar was born and raised in the Chicago suburbs. He is currently a sales account manager with the UCA Group, and resides in St. Charles, Illinois.

"I am strong when I am on your shoulders.
You raise me up to more than I can be."

"You Raise Me Up," lyrics by Brendan Graham

– 45 –

Father and Son As One

the story of Dick and Rick Hoyt

A despicable pair ruined the 2013 Boston Marathon. They took lives. They grabbed headlines.

A father-son pair ran the 2013 Boston Marathon. They inspired lives. They deserved headlines.

Since 1977, Dick and Rick Hoyt, or "Team Hoyt," have competed in over 1000 endurance events. This was their 31st Boston Marathon together. The duo has also completed six Ironman competitions, perhaps the toughest of all athletic challenges.

Dick, the dad, is 73. Rick is 51. Impressive enough. But that's not all. Rick is a quadriplegic. He's had cerebral palsy since birth. He lives in a wheelchair. He speaks with the help of a computer.

He "runs" with Dad's legs. Dad pushes, pulls, pedals and carries Rick all the way.

As father and son. As one.

One of Team Hoyt's first races together

It started in 1977, when Rick was a kid. He wanted to take part in a 5-mile race to raise money for a paralyzed athlete. Dick pushed Rick's wheelchair every inch of the course. They finished second to last.

At the end of that race, Rick said to Dad, "When I'm running, it feels like I'm not handicapped."

Since that day, Dick vowed to help his son feel handicapped no more. Dick and Rick not only compete together. They biked and ran across the U.S. in 1992. That was the year before Rick graduated from Boston College, another milestone.

Rick and Dick Hoyt, still going strong

In a triathlon, Dick bungees a small boat, holding his son, for the swimming stage. When they bike, the duo share a special two-seater. For running, Dick pushes Rick in a custom-made running chair.

"Rick," someone once asked, "if you could give Dad one thing, what would it be?"

"The thing I'd most like is for my dad to sit in the chair and I would push him."

About the Contributor

Rick and Dick Hoyt had to stop a mile short of the Boston Marathon finish line in 2013 because of the bomb explosions. A bystander gave them a ride back to their hotel. Rick's

wheelchair had to be left behind, but was found and returned the next day.

*"When most people are done,
my work has just begun ...."*

Aaron Greenlee

– 46 –

Meticularity

by Greg Hague

In 1960, I was just 12, but scrounging for cash. I longed for a Weatherby 300 Magnum rifle. I had a vision of hunting Kodiak bears in the wilds of Alaska. Go figure.

Chubby saw a savvy parenting opportunity. He offered me a job as "Assistant to Aaron." Aaron was the janitor for our family real estate firm.

Chubby said he wanted me to know what a "real job" was like and, as he said, "how to live the Big M." Big M, I wondered?

Aaron was a stocky, middle-aged black man with shiny white teeth and a smile of gold. Everyone loved Aaron.

Aaron's "room" was a plywood enclosure in the office basement. His small, black metal desk shined like a penny. The top drawer was perfect as pie. The surface was neat as a nut, with photos of family, and a picture of Dad.

My first job was to shine up the wood. The interior walls of our building were paneled in cherry wood. The desks were mahogany. The place was stunning. Dad was so proud. So was Aaron.

I dusted and shined. Gave it my best. Worked all day buffing that wood. And, that's how I learned about the Big M.

Aaron came by to check out my work. "Not bad," he said, "but not all that good."

Not all that good, I thought (but thankfully didn't say it to Aaron).

Aaron showed me around. I had missed a little smudge here and a tiny spot there. He was right. It wasn't that bad. It just wasn't that good.

That evening at dinner, Chubby asked about my day. I told him what happened. Here's what he said,

Aaron with Greg's horse, Penny

"Aaron may be the janitor, but he's the best mentor I have. This man is a beacon of doing it right.

With Aaron, good is never good enough. Strive for perfection, then up it from there. Where others leave off, Aaron digs in. Aaron leads more than a *meticulous* life. It's a life of METICULARITY. That's the Big M."

I reflect back on my dad and his mentor named Aaron. I understand now.

The Big M is why Chubby stayed up all night to write real estate ads. It's why his contracts were models of clarity and legally right.

From the drawer in his dresser, to the trunk of his car, to the business he ran, Dad lived the Big M. Good was never good enough. This he learned from Aaron, his janitor, friend, and mentor.

The Big M has made an astounding difference in my life. Little things, like when others push "send" on emails, texts, and blog posts—I remember the Big M, and take a last look. Extra hours prepping for meetings, talks, and meaningful calls. If I can't beat 'em with skill, I'll smoke 'em by knowing it all.

Aaron was with us the rest of his life. Dad's company flourished into one of the largest in town. At Aaron's final goodbye, Dad gave the talk. His words about Aaron I'll never forget. Of all the people he knew, other than Mom, Aaron was the key to his success.

Dad's last words when he delivered Aaron's eulogy:

"When you think you're now done, you've only begun."

"Preach the gospel every day,
and if necessary use words."

Saint Francis of Assisi

– 47 –
Do The Right Thing
contributed by Dale Brown

I guess you could say that my story of faith started two days before I was born.

My so-called father—I've always referred to him as "my mother's husband"—left my mother, two young sisters (11 and 12 years of age), and me, and he never returned. His departure put my mother in a difficult position.

She had an eighth-grade education, came off the farm in North Dakota, and couldn't get a job during the Great Depression in 1935. In the cold prairies of North Dakota, she had to do two things that were very unpleasant for her. She became a babysitter to earn money, and she had to put our family on welfare.

We lived in a one-room apartment above a bar and hardware store, and I remember my mother getting $42.50 in Ward County welfare each month. She sat down and meticulously decided what breads and canned goods we could buy for the coming week.

Several times during these difficult times, my mother taught me a lesson that has stayed with me during my entire life.

Two times, I saw my mother get on her winter coat, walk down a flight of stairs, and take back to the Red Owl and the Piggly Wiggly grocery stores 25¢ and 40¢ because the clerks had given her too much change for the groceries she'd brought home.

Seeing her dressing in the middle of winter, I said, "Mama, where are you going?" She said, "Oh, I'm taking this money back to the store. They gave me too much change."

It reminds me of a poem by Edgar Guest:

I'd rather *see* a lesson than hear one any day.

I'd rather you walk with me than to merely show the way.

The eye is a better teacher, and more willing than the ear.

And counsel is confusing but example's always clear.

The best of all the teachers are the ones who live the creed.

To see good put into action is what everybody needs.

I soon can learn to do it if you let me see it done.

I can see your hand in action, but your tongue too fast may run.

And the counsel you are giving may be very fine and true,

But I'd rather get my lessons by observing what you do.

My mother followed the advice of St. Francis of Assisi in the 13th century when he said, "Preach the gospel every day, and if necessary use words."

I saw other lessons in the life of this woman who had no PhD behind her name. Not once, after being abandoned, did I hear my mother talk negatively about the man who had walked out on us and never returned, never sent any money, never wrote.

She didn't drink, and she never smoked. I never heard her swear. She was never bitter or angry, and she never complained about her situation in life.

My mother taught me a great deal of things, but most of all she taught me to treasure each day of life and, when in doubt, simply do the right thing.

ABOUT THE CONTRIBUTOR

Louisiana State University basketball coach Dale Brown accomplished what most do not. "The Coach" became the remarkable man he aspired to be. Louisiana Legend. Basketball Hall of Fame Coach. SEC Coach of the Year. TV and radio analyst. Author. Speaker. Movie Consultant.

Coach Brown attributes his success to his mom, who stepped in with a fatherly hand after her husband left the family. She was breadwinner, nurturer, and mentor, and her son Dale is grateful for the example she set.

*"To be trusted is a greater compliment
than being loved."*

George MacDonald

– 48 –

Example of Trust

contributed by David Horsager

When I was about ten, my dad and I were in the bean fields checking the irrigators on our farm in North Central Minnesota. Between fields, Dad stopped the pickup, spotting a bit of trash in the road.

David Horsager and his father, Clarence

I was always taught to help keep the land clean, so I opened my door, reached out and picked up the trash. It was a *Playboy* magazine. Without a word, Dad swiped it away and stashed it under the seat.

We drove from field to field, from irrigator to irrigator. We said not a word.

I thought about what Dad had so often said. That kind of stuff was harmful and bad. It encouraged disrespect for women. It could hurt your marriage. It was a first step down a very low road.

Once we got home, Dad went to the workshop. I helped Mom in the house. A bit later, I found myself peering out the window toward the workshop. I could see my dad well. He could not see me.

I watched as Dad pulled himself out from under the tractor and walked to the truck. He reached under the seat and fished out the magazine. Then, without glancing down for a second, he strode over to our shop stove and

On the McCormick-Deering tractor Clarence used as a kid

unceremoniously tossed that *Playboy* into the fire. He had no idea I was watching.

My trust in Dad was put to the test that day. He aced it with stars. That was only the start. I watched him walk what he talked and live what he taught, year after year.

How many fathers would have taken a peek? It might not seem like much, but to me it said all. My dad was an example of trust. He stood incredibly tall. Thanks to a dad I could trust, I wrote a bestselling book and teach the power of trust throughout the world today.

ABOUT THE CONTRIBUTOR

David Horsager, MA, CSP, is the author of the *Wall Street Journal* bestselling business/leadership book, *The Trust Edge: How Top Leaders Gain Faster Results, Deeper Relationships, and A Stronger Bottom Line.* He is also an entrepreneur, professor, and award-winning keynote speaker. His work has been featured in *Fast Company*, *Forbes*, the *New York Post*, *SUCCESS* magazine, and more.

Clarence Horsager with his grandkids, Vanessa and Isaiah, in the corn truck

*"Beauty is not in the face;
beauty is a light in the heart."*

Kahlil Gibran

— 49 —

Beauty and the Beast

contributed by Pat McMahon

I'm sure you know the story of "Beauty and the Beast." But what you probably don't know is … I'm their son.

No, I don't mean the couple in the children's story. But, it would have been perfectly appropriate to call my parents Beauty and the Beast because that's the way they talked about themselves.

You see, before my father and mother met and went into the entertainment business, my dad was a prizefighter, a professional boxer with over 90 fights. Back in those days, they didn't check

Pat teaching his dad, Jack, a thing or two

Young Pat's smile (left) and his antics with his dad (above) offer a glimpse into the fun-loving life of the McMahon family

personal information very carefully, so he was able to get into the fight game when he was 14 years old.

He had a pretty impressive record too, but it was at the expense of his face, layers of scar tissue that built up on his brow, a nose broken so many times it spread in multiple directions. How he ever heard anything through the tiny pinholes of his "cauliflower" ears is a wonder.

And then there was my mom, The Beauty. She was the essence of the song "Tiny Dancer."

Mom was a petite ballerina, a tap dancer, a skilled acrobat. She attracted everyone, but she loved The Beast. And did he ever love her!

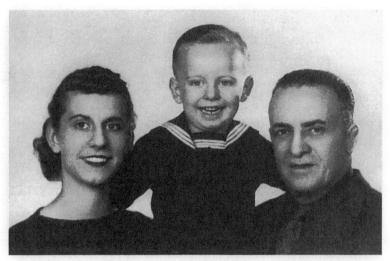

Pat with his mother and father, Beauty and the Beast

They never minded showing it either, mostly by just being real. They were always openly honest with one another about their feelings.

For my father, that meant a surprising level of tenderness and sensitivity, about so many things, which has allowed me to keep and cherish this portrait of him.

Here was a man whose appearance translated, to many, as a rough-hewn, tough-as-nails, street guy, someone to be wary of, perhaps to avoid, someone for whom sentimentality was probably a weakness.

But my real life memory is, and always will be, of a role model: orphaned at 10, who regularly wept in appreciation of all things beautiful, from ballet, to animal stories, to my mother.

My mother, The Beauty, who loved nothing more than softly kissing that broken nose on the magnificent face of The Beast.

From them I learned the truth of these words by Kahlil Gibran: "Beauty is not in the face; beauty is a light in the heart."

About the Contributor

Pat McMahon is a legend in Arizona broadcasting. His 30 years on the long-running, groundbreaking children's show "Wallace and Ladmo" are just part of his remarkable resume, which includes acting, producing, writing, and recording. Pat's professional and personal contributions have been recognized with seven Emmy awards, major national and international radio awards, and numerous civic, educational and humanitarian awards.

Pat and his wife, Duffy, the love of his life

> *"A lot of people get so hung up on what they say they can't have that they don't think for a second about whether they really want it."*
>
> Lionel Shriver

– 50 –

Do You Know About Vacuums?

contributed by Megan Murphy-Porth

Dad raised me from nine. Mom left us that year. My brother, Ryan, was just seven. Those were tough times.

We did have one bit of luck. Dad won a trip to Hawaii. The catch? Tickets for two. He'll probably take Ryan, I thought.

Wrong. Dad asked me along!

Me and my dad. A trip with just him. Right after Mom left. You can't know what that meant.

Dad and I spent a week doing it all. We inspected

Megan in Hawaii

each beach. We examined each shell. We ate off the same plate. We even toured the Dole pineapple factory, my hand tucked tightly in his.

On our last day, we walked to the beach and decided to chill. Well, "chill" might not be exactly right. Over and over, I'd jump off Dad's shoulders into the sea. Snorkeling. Splash fights. So wild and fun.

As we swam in the warm, crystalline blue, Dad casually asked, "Megan, have you learned about vacuums yet?"

My first thought? Vacuums were for sweeping the floor. Was Dad adding a task to my chores? He read the look on my face.

"No," Dad laughed, "Like a vacuum in space?"

Megan and her dad on graduation day

I shrugged. "Well," said Dad, "In space, there's cosmic stuff we call mass." I was intrigued.

"In space, mass detests a void. It rushes to fill that vacuum all up. A good example is called a black hole."

I nodded for him to go on.

"Well," said Dad, "People are just like that. They instinctively rush to fill voids. It's true even when they know they could likely be hurt. They just can't resist. For example, have you ever noticed, when something is hard to get, you want it that much more? Or, if someone doesn't want to be your friend, you want them as a friend even more?"

I thought for a second. It had happened to me.

Dad continued, "You wanted that person, not because of who they were, but because they didn't want you. They created a negative vacuum. You were sucked in.

"So, when you find yourself attracted to a person, a deal or a thing, ask yourself, is it really the vacuum?"

A long pause. "Daddy, I'm not sure I understand ...."

My father smiled and said, "Someday you will." He pushed me back into the water. We continued to play.

That someday is now. It was some of the best advice I've ever heard.

Surround yourself with true friends. Make decisions to act and to buy based on real merit. Don't rush to a vacuum. Don't get sucked in.

What else did I learn? I have a very smart dad!

About the Contributor

Megan Murphy-Porth recently graduated from Phoenix School of Law. She is married to Michael Porth and has two beautiful daughters.

Megan and husband, Michael, show the love to Megan's dad, Rick, at their wedding

"Son, things in life will go bad. And while you can't change that, you can have a back-up plan."
Bob Gomlicker

– 51 –

Mr. Back-Up Plan

contributed by Mike Gomlicker

My name is Mike Gomlicker. My dad's name is Bob. He won't bore you with chatter, meaningless talk. Those words were his best. They define who Dad is.

Air Force combat pilot. Commercial airline captain. My father held lives in his hands during those years. In my dad's hands is a great place to be.

Emergency time? Cool and calm. Quick to react. Dad responds in a flash like bad was the plan.

He's told me stories. Things that happened. Fathers and sons, daughters and moms, innocent lives in his care.

But Dad thought ahead. Whatever went wrong, he knew what to do. While others relaxed and daydreamed before a long flight, Dad would go think, somewhere alone.

He taught me to follow this plan with all that I do. Go somewhere away from the rest. Think everything through.

What could go wrong? What would I do? Dad had a back-up plan for anything from a ruptured wing to a broken toilet. Dad knew what to do.

Bob Gomlicker boarding his T-38

Dad taught me how to live an exciting, adventurous life. And do it safely.

What could go wrong? "Think it through in advance," he'd say. Have a back-up plan.

Triathlete. Hunter. Fisher. Explorer. Pilot. World traveler. Live off the land. Multiple hats. Numerous skills. Mr. Back-Up Plan. That's my dad.

Here's an example of how Dad taught me this valuable rule:

A trip into the remote Alaskan wild. No phones. No way to get home. Live off the land.

A bush plane dropped us in a remote location along the Kisaralik River. It would return, but not for a week!

We were alone. No Hawaiian vacation this time. It was Dad's way of teaching. It was a lesson on thinking ahead,

Above: Bob with sons, Bryan and Michael, at the Iron Kids competition

Left: Iron Kid winners—all the things this trio learned in the Alaskan wild were good preparation

having back-up plans, and learning what to do when things went bad.

We fished for our food, but my father always had some freeze-dried in case the fish didn't bite—a back-up plan.

We routinely saw grizzlies just across the river. "If one ever grabs your fish, cut the line, but don't run." A back-up plan.

Attacked by a bear? Dad had a gun. It was not to be touched, no shooting game. A back-up plan.

I could write a book on what I learned from that trip alone (there were many more). The bottom line?

Have a back-up plan. That was the point.

My dad. Mr. Back-up Plan.

About the Contributor

Mike Gomlicker lives in Scottsdale, Arizona. He is studying to obtain his General Contractor license. Mike has a special gift. He can fix anything that breaks. Anything.

Father and son at sea

"As we express our gratitude, we must never forget that the highest appreciation is not to utter words, but to live by them."

John F. Kennedy

– 52 –

Dads Need Their Kids

by Greg Hague

Dad was proud. So was I.

I had worked hard to stand on that stage.

May 1974. Washington D.C. Law school graduation. What a magnificent day.

I felt like I'd made it in life. Such innocence. It makes me smile today. The ceremony concluded. Chubby left with me. I drove. We were alone.

My dad was normally a talkative man. Not that day. Strange. We drove blocks without saying a word. He then looked over and said, "Greg, would you like to stop for a snack?"

I said, "Sure, why not?" I was always up for a snack.

We sat in a booth at a small M Street café. Memories of those Saturday mornings together at Perkins Pancake House in earlier days. Pie and iced tea sounded nice that hot afternoon. Dad seemed edgy, something was not right. Fidgety, restless, uneasy, this was not the father I knew.

Chubby slowly stirred sugar into his tea, looking not at the tea, but rather at me.

Could I ever have known what would come next? Not if I'd had a lifetime to guess. I was seconds away from a punch in the gut. I would soon learn the man I adored was hurting inside, joyous for me, but sad in a way.

Chubby started to speak, but suddenly stopped. He picked up his napkin. I could see the water glistening in his eyes. He dabbed off a bit of moisture from high on one cheek. I distinctly remember what flashed in my mind. On this day of celebration, what could be wrong?

Chubby took a deep breath and said something like this,

"Greg, you've just accomplished what I never could.

"College was no option for me. Law school would have been a laughable dream.

"I didn't have grades. I didn't have money. I lost my dad when I was just three.

"Since the day of your birth, I wanted you to reach heights I never could. I'm so proud of you."

I suddenly had watery eyes too. Really, I welled up. It sounds stupid, but in the middle of that restaurant, I was dripping tears on the pie in my plate.

Chubby lost his dad at age 3

This man was responsible for what, at this point, was the most magnificent day of my life. He got me there. He was my mentor, my friend, my #1 cheerleader. He was proud of me? I was about to say how proud I was of him. How thankful, too.

What came next, I could never have known. Did you ever see a dad's joy make a son sad? Chubby spoke before I could.

"Greg, you will be welcomed by people and groups who would not accept me. As an attorney, an educated man, you are a person they will look up to. I've dreamed that one day you would command the respect I never could."

I got it. This had never occurred to me. Dad hadn't come from the right side of the tracks. Our city had circles of old money — inheritance-rich, blue-blooded men. Chubby was not one of them.

He'd worked for his bucks. He'd beat the streets. He'd labored into the night. He was not one of those country club elite. Dad had been spurned by these "important" men. I hadn't known. Cincinnati, Ohio, could be a very mean town.

What did I learn at the M Street Café? A father's support and advice had made my life great. Now, I was determined to reciprocate.

I committed to make Dad understand how important he was. To me. To everyone. When I was done, he'd realize those blue-bloods weren't worthy to shine his shoes. To this day, I've never joined one of those "elite" clubs. If Chubby wasn't good enough for them, they aren't good enough for his son. Dad, that's a tribute to you.

What did I learn at the M Street Café? We know kids need their dads. Sometimes, dads need their kids.

Exploring caves in Hawaii, Greg's boys needed him then ...

... and today they all need each other

– Conclusion –

Man Up
or Wimp Out

Where do you want to be in three years? What will stop you? Based on my experience, it's not what you think.

Don't know what to do? Bet you do.

Don't have money? It's an excuse—if you have the right idea, the work ethic, and the courage to ask, the money will come.

Hard work? You'd bust your butt if you knew that this alone would get it done.

So what is it? What's the big stopper? What's going to screw up your dream?

If you're honest with yourself, down deep you know. It's you. You don't have the guts to do what it takes.

Don't be offended. It's what stops most people.

When I reflect back on the single most significant thing I learned from my dad, the one thing that stands out above the rest, it was doing the uncomfortable. Doing the stressful. Swimming in strange waters. Making difficult calls. Facing difficult people. Going where no one knew me, and I knew not a soul.

Did I always do right? Sadly, no. I was simply not willing to risk rejection, failure and embarrassment. It was so dumb. I had nothing to lose. I just didn't see it. Every time I wimped out, I was opening a door for someone else to step in. Stupid!

It's smart to be afraid of playing Russian roulette. There's nothing to gain. It could cost you your life.

But the fear of embarrassment, rejection and failure are illogical, no-downside fears. You have nothing to lose but a mental bruise.

Take it from my dad, Chubby. If you look back with disappointment in three years, it was likely your fear. You were solely to blame. Wimpy. Gutless. You ran with the herd instead of having the courage to make yourself heard.

Man up. Make yourself heard.

—GREG HAGUE, The Savvy Dad

ABOUT THE AUTHOR

Greg Hague (The Savvy Dad) has worn many hats. Serial entrepreneur. Attorney. Law professor. Real estate developer. Author. Speaker. Pilot. And of course, being a dad to his three sons and nephew.

Anyone who knows Greg will attest that he operates at one speed—full tilt. He's a "go for it" kind of guy. His defining quality is his passion for whatever he does.

Greg's endeavors have been the subject of articles and interviews in newspapers, magazines, and on radio and television shows from coast to coast, including the *Wall Street Journal, U.S. New & World Report*, *MONEY* magazine, National Public Radio, Inman News, *REALTOR* magazine, and Kiplinger's book, *Buying and Selling a Home*.

Greg plays and travels as hard as he works, motorcycling throughout the U.S., as well as Mexico, Canada, Europe, and South Africa. He's landed his single engine plane on remote Bahamian beaches and in the Baja backcountry.

Greg refers to Roseann as the "light of my life" and "the woman who made me a better man." He is especially proud of his nephew and sons, who are each embracing their passions, one in music, one as an entrepreneur, one as a top level corporate manager, and the youngest following his dad's footsteps in the law.

Greg commented, "At the end of my days, when my friends and family remember me, I hope it will be as a good husband, a great father, and a true friend."

Greg and Roseann live in Scottsdale, Arizona, and Alpine, Wyoming, with the world's best dogs, Tanner and Chubby.

A Round of Applause

A famous proverb reads, "It takes a community to raise a child." It has taken a community to help grow this baby of mine.

This book would not have been possible without the heartfelt tributes by sons and daughters to their savvy dads. My sincere appreciation to each of you for entrusting me with your memories, stories, and families.

First, I'd like to thank my friend **Christopher Neck** for being my right hand in brainstorming and writing this book. He is the single best source of remarkable "dad" stories in the universe. He's a professor, author, incredible dad, and really nice guy. He works nonstop and writes like Hemingway. Whatever needs doing, Chris does it 10+. There would be no book without Chris. And, Chris brought us Elizabeth.

Thank you to **Elizabeth Parsons** for her tireless efforts in helping to find and compose the stories for this book. She is one of the most talented writers, hardest workers, and nicest people I've ever known.

I'd be nowhere without **Pat Veriepe**. Nice? They don't make people with better hearts. Talented? She's been my "go to" from day one. She manages the website, the blog and the national emails. She lays out the stories, proofs the copy, and suggests improvements in every area. When I go to sleep, Pat is still at it.

Katie Rose Cunin is my niece. Without her, there would be no book. She pulled everything together. What you see is her magnificent work ... the organization, the editing, the presentation, the look. I have three sons. If I could choose a daughter, Katie Rose would be the one (if she'd consent to have me as a savvy dad).

A very special thanks to **Erika Bentley**, who so brilliantly designed the cover for this book. Her creativity and graphic design skills are among the best I've observed over 40 years in business. And she is a dream to work with. Erika, you are fantastic!

We launched the book. It took off. The first edition received over 50 five-star reviews the first month. We decided to produce an enhanced, full-color version with over 200 family photos to complement the stories. We needed help.

Melanie Jongsma to the rescue! Her talent and expertise created a new edition second to none. The photo editing, layout, and Melanie's long, late-night hours made this better than we had even imagined (and we have good imaginations).

Brian Hague, my oldest son. He's managed the project since day one. Whatever needs doing, he does better than I ever could. And, he's a gifted writer, to boot—of stories and music. A world-class musician, Brian's new song (and video) "Go Gettas" is as good as you've ever heard. A father working with his talented son? I'm one very lucky savvy dad.

And Roseann? The light of my life. My partner in all that I do. She taught me to write. She made me nice. She keeps me straight. She edits and improves every word of every story before it goes out. She makes my life in every way. And, she's a savvy mom like you can't believe.

—GREG HAGUE